Business Leadership
And
Motivation

:: Author ::

RAJESHKUMAR A. SHRIMALI
(M.COM, B.ED, UGC NET, M.PHIL)

Published By

Green Flag Foundation
Sabarkantha, Gujrat-383210, India.
www.eternityzxy.com

ISBN 978-93-83579-61-7

First Publication: January 2014

Copyright: Author
      (c) *RAJESHKUMAR A. SHRIMALI*

ISBN 978-93-83579-61-7

Price: Rs.170/-

Published by: Green Flag Foundation
      Sabarkantha, Gujrat-383210, India

Business Leadership And Motivation

Content

Part : I Business Leadership Basics

●What is Leadership ●Characteristics of Leadership ●Importance of Leadership ●Role of a Leader ●Qualities of a Leader ●Leadership and Management - Relationship & Differences ●Differences between Leadership and Management ● Leader versus Manager ●Authority v/s Leadership ●Leadership and Motivation ●Emotional Intelligence for Leaders ●Organizational Leadership ●Leadership Ethics - Traits of an Ethical Leader ●Leadership Strategy - Which Leadership Style to Follow ? ●Leadership Styles - Important Leadership Styles ●How to Create a Personal Leadership Brand ? ●Level 5 Leadership ●Situational Leadership - Meaning and Concept ●Impact of Situational Leadership on Performance and Motivation ●Introduction to Leadership Development ●Leadership: Intrinsic v/s Extrinsic Motivation ●Leadership for the 21st Century ●Three Traits of Effective Leadership ●Social Stratification and Hierarchy: What Business Leaders Ought to Know ●Hierarchy and its uses and disadvantages ●Be Global in Attitude yet Local in Execution ●The Elements of Leadership in Adversity ●The Characteristics of Leadership in Adversity ●Leadership Theories - Important Theories of Leadership ●Transformational Leadership Theory ●Implications of Transactional Theory ●Difference between Transactional and Transformational Leaders ●Continuum of Leadership Behaviour ●Likert's Management System ●Leadership and Trust ●How to be a Good Leader - What makes Leadership Effective ? ●Effective Leadership Skills - What it takes to be an Effective Leader ●Leadership Vision ●Different Types of Power ●Women and Leadership ●What are the Challenges in Leadership ? ●Tips to Overcome Challenges in Leadership ●Role of Communication in Overcoming Leadership Challenges ●Role of Management/Organization in Overcoming Leadership Challenges

Part : II Motivation

●What is Motivation ? ●Maslow's Need Hierarchy Model ●Motivation Incentives - Incentives to motivate employees ●Importance of Motivation ●Staff Motivation - Motivation Tips for Employees ●Self Motivation at Work ●Team Motivation - Tips for Motivating Team ●The Role of

Motivation in Organizational Behavior ●Essentials / Features of a Good Motivation System ●Classical Theories of Motivation ●Maslow's Hierarchy of Needs Theory ●Implications of Maslow's Hierarchy of Needs Theory for Managers ●Limitations of Maslow's Theory ●Herzberg's Two-Factor Theory of Motivation ●Limitations of Two-Factor Theory ●Implications of Two-Factor Theory ●Theory X and Theory Y ●Implications of Theory X and Theory Y ●Modern Theories of Motivation ●ERG Theory ●Implications of the ERG Theory ●Expectancy Theory of Motivation ●Implications of the Expectancy Theory ●McClelland's Theory of Needs ●Goal Setting Theory of Motivation ●Advantages of Goal Setting Theory ●Limitations of Goal Setting Theory ●Reinforcement Theory of Motivation ●McClelland's Theory of Needs ●Reinforcement Theory of Motivation ●Implications of Reinforcement Theory ●Equity Theory of Motivation ●Assumptions of the Equity Theory ●Expectancy Theory of Motivation ●Advantages of the Expectancy Theory ●Limitations of the Expectancy Theory ●Implications of the Expectancy Theory

———————

Part : I
Business Leadership Basics

- **What is Leadership**

  Leadership is a process by which an executive can direct, guide and influence the behavior and work of others towards accomplishment of specific goals in a given situation. Leadership is the ability of a manager to induce the subordinates to work with confidence and zeal.

  Leadership is the potential to influence behaviour of others. It is also defined as the capacity to influence a group towards the realization of a goal. Leaders are required to develop future visions, and to motivate the organizational members to want to achieve the visions.

  According to Keith Davis, "Leadership is the ability to persuade others to seek defined objectives enthusiastically. It is the human factor which binds a group together and motivates it towards goals."

- **Characteristics of Leadership**
  1. It is a inter-personal process in which a manager is into influencing and guiding workers towards attainment of goals.
  2. It denotes a few qualities to be present in a person which includes intelligence, maturity and personality.
  3. It is a group process. It involves two or more people interacting with each other.
  4. A leader is involved in shaping and moulding the behaviour of the group towards accomplishment of organizational goals.
  5. Leadership is situation bound. There is no best style of leadership. It all depends upon tackling with the situations.

- **Importance of Leadership**

  Leadership is an important function of management which helps to maximize efficiency and to achieve organizational goals. The following points justify the importance of leadership in a concern.
  1. **Initiates action-** Leader is a person who starts the work by communicating the policies and plans to the subordinates from where the work actually starts.
  2. **Motivation-** A leader proves to be playing an incentive role in the concern's working. He motivates the employees with economic and non-economic rewards and thereby gets the work from the subordinates.

2

3. **Providing guidance-** A leader has to not only supervise but also play a guiding role for the subordinates. Guidance here means instructing the subordinates the way they have to perform their work effectively and efficiently.

4. **Creating confidence-** Confidence is an important factor which can be achieved through expressing the work efforts to the subordinates, explaining them clearly their role and giving them guidelines to achieve the goals effectively. It is also important to hear the employees with regards to their complaints and problems.

5. **Building morale-** Morale denotes willing co-operation of the employees towards their work and getting them into confidence and winning their trust. A leader can be a morale booster by achieving full co-operation so that they perform with best of their abilities as they work to achieve goals.

6. **Builds work environment-** Management is getting things done from people. An efficient work environment helps in sound and stable growth. Therefore, human relations should be kept into mind by a leader. He should have personal contacts with employees and should listen to their problems and solve them. He should treat employees on humanitarian terms.

7. **Co-ordination-** Co-ordination can be achieved through reconciling personal interests with organizational goals. This synchronization can be achieved through proper and effective co-ordination which should be primary motive of a leader.

- **Role of a Leader**

Following are the main roles of a leader in an organization :

1. **Required at all levels-** Leadership is a function which is important at all levels of management. In the top level, it is important for getting co-operation in formulation of plans and policics. In the middle and lower level, it is required for interpretation and execution of plans and programmes framed by the top management. Leadership can be exercised through guidance and counseling of the subordinates at the time of execution of plans.

2. **Representative of the organization-** A leader, i.e., a manager is said to be the representative of the enterprise. He has to represent

the concern at seminars, conferences, general meetings, etc. His role is to communicate the rationale of the enterprise to outside public. He is also representative of the own department which he leads.

3. **Integrates and reconciles the personal goals with organizational goals-** A leader through leadership traits helps in reconciling/ integrating the personal goals of the employees with the organizational goals. He is trying to co-ordinate the efforts of people towards a common purpose and thereby achieves objectives. This can be done only if he can influence and get willing co-operation and urge to accomplish the objectives.

4. **He solicits support-** A leader is a manager and besides that he is a person who entertains and invites support and co- operation of subordinates. This he can do by his personality, intelligence, maturity and experience which can provide him positive result. In this regard, a leader has to invite suggestions and if possible implement them into plans and programmes of enterprise. This way, he can solicit full support of employees which results in willingness to work and thereby effectiveness in running of a concern.

5. **As a friend, philosopher and guide-** A leader must possess the three dimensional traits in him. He can be a friend by sharing the feelings, opinions and desires with the employees. He can be a philosopher by utilizing his intelligence and experience and thereby guiding the employees as and when time requires. He can be a guide by supervising and communicating the employees the plans and policies of top management and secure their co-operation to achieve the goals of a concern. At times he can also play the role of a counselor by counseling and a problem-solving approach. He can listen to the problems of the employees and try to solve them.

- **Qualities of a Leader**
  A leader has got multidimensional traits in him which makes him appealing and effective in behavior. The following are the requisites to be present in a good leader:

4

1. **Physical appearance-** A leader must have a pleasing appearance. Physique and health are very important for a good leader.

2. **Vision and foresight-** A leader cannot maintain influence unless he exhibits that he is forward looking. He has to visualize situations and thereby has to frame logical programmes.

3. **Intelligence-** A leader should be intelligent enough to examine problems and difficult situations. He should be analytical who weighs pros and cons and then summarizes the situation. Therefore, a positive bent of mind and mature outlook is very important.

4. **Communicative skills-** A leader must be able to communicate the policies and procedures clearly, precisely and effectively. This can be helpful in persuasion and stimulation.

5. **Objective-** A leader has to be having a fair outlook which is free from bias and which does not reflects his willingness towards a particular individual. He should develop his own opinion and should base his judgement on facts and logic.

6. **Knowledge of work-** A leader should be very precisely knowing the nature of work of his subordinates because it is then he can win the trust and confidence of his subordinates.

7. **Sense of responsibility-** Responsibility and accountability towards an individual's work is very important to bring a sense of influence. A leader must have a sense of responsibility towards organizational goals because only then he can get maximum of capabilities exploited in a real sense. For this, he has to motivate himself and arouse and urge to give best of his abilities. Only then he can motivate the subordinates to the best.

8. **Self-confidence and will-power-** Confidence in himself is important to earn the confidence of the subordinates. He should be trustworthy and should handle the situations with full will power. (You can read more about Self-Confidence at : Self Confidence - Tips to be Confident and Eliminate Your Apprehensions).

9. **Humanist-**This trait to be present in a leader is essential because he deals with human beings and is in personal contact with them. He has to handle the personal problems of his subordinates with great care and attention. Therefore, treating the human beings on

humanitarian grounds is essential for building a congenial environment.

10. **Empathy-** It is an old adage "Stepping into the shoes of others". This is very important because fair judgement and objectivity comes only then. A leader should understand the problems and complaints of employees and should also have a complete view of the needs and aspirations of the employees. This helps in improving human relations and personal contacts with the employees.

From the above qualities present in a leader, one can understand the scope of leadership and it's importance for scope of business. A leader cannot have all traits at one time. But a few of them helps in achieving effective results.

- **Leadership and Management - Relationship & Differences**

Leadership and management are the terms that are often considered synonymous. It is essential to understand that leadership is an essential part of effective management. As a crucial component of management, remarkable leadership behaviour stresses upon building an environment in which each and every employee develops and excels. Leadership is defined as the potential to influence and drive the group efforts towards the accomplishment of goals. This influence may originate from formal sources, such as that provided by acquisition of managerial position in an organization.

A manager must have traits of a leader, i.e., he must possess leadership qualities. Leaders develop and begin strategies that build and sustain competitive advantage. Organizations require robust leadership and robust management for optimal organizational efficiency.

- **Differences between Leadership and Management**

Leadership differs from management in a sense that:

1. While managers lay down the structure and delegates authority and responsibility, leaders provides direction by developing the organizational vision and communicating it to the employees and inspiring them to achieve it.

6

2. While management includes focus on planning, organizing, staffing, directing and controlling; leadership is mainly a part of directing function of management. Leaders focus on listening, building relationships, teamwork, inspiring, motivating and persuading the followers.

3. While a leader gets his authority from his followers, a manager gets his authority by virtue of his position in the organization.

4. While managers follow the organization's policies and procedure, the leaders follow their own instinct.

5. Management is more of science as the managers are exact, planned, standard, logical and more of mind. Leadership, on the other hand, is an art. In an organization, if the managers are required, then leaders are a must/essential.

6. While management deals with the technical dimension in an organization or the job content; leadership deals with the people aspect in an organization.

7. While management measures/evaluates people by their name, past records, present performance; leadership sees and evaluates individuals as having potential for things that can't be measured, i.e., it deals with future and the performance of people if their potential is fully extracted.

8. If management is reactive, leadership is proactive.

9. Management is based more on written communication, while leadership is based more on verbal communication.

The organizations which are over managed and under-led do not perform upto the benchmark. **Leadership accompanied by management sets a new direction and makes efficient use of resources to achieve it**. Both leadership and management are essential for individual as well as organizational success.

- **Leader versus Manager**

    "Leadership and managership are two synonymous terms" is an incorrect statement. Leadership doesn't require any managerial position to act as a leader. On the other hand, a manager can be a true manager only if he has got the traits of leader in him. By virtue of his position, manager has to provide leadership to his group. A manager has to perform all five functions to achieve goals, i.e., <u>Planning</u>, <u>Organizing</u>, Staffing, <u>Directing</u>, and Controlling. Leadership is a part of these functions. Leadership as a general term is not related to managership. A person can be a leader by virtue of qualities in him. For example: leader of a club, class, welfare association, social organization, etc. Therefore, it is true to say that, "All managers are leaders, but all leaders are not managers."

A leader is one who influences the behavior and work of others in group efforts towards achievement of specified goals in a given situation. On the other hand, manager can be a true manager only if he has got traits of leader in him. Manager at all levels are expected to be the leaders of work groups so that subordinates willingly carry instructions and accept their guidance. A person can be a leader by virtue of all qualities in him.

Leaders and Managers can be compared on the following basis:

Basis	Manager	Leader
Origin	A person becomes a manager by virtue of his position.	A person becomes a leader on basis of his personal qualities.
Formal Rights	Manager has got formal rights in an organization because of his status.	Rights are not available to a leader.
Followers	The subordinates are the followers of managers.	The group of employees whom the leaders leads are his followers.
Functions	A manager performs all five functions of management.	Leader influences people to work willingly for group objectives.
Necessity	A manager is very essential to a concern.	A leader is required to create cordial relation

		between person working in and for organization.
Stability	It is more stable.	Leadership is temporary.
Mutual Relationship	All managers are leaders.	All leaders are not managers.
Accountability	Manager is accountable for self and subordinates behaviour and performance.	Leaders have no well defined accountability.
Concern	A manager's concern is organizational goals.	A leader's concern is group goals and member's satisfaction.
Followers	People follow manager by virtue of job description.	People follow them on voluntary basis.
Role continuation	A manager can continue in office till he performs his duties satisfactorily in congruence with organizational goals.	A leader can maintain his position only through day to day wishes of followers.
Sanctions	Manager has command over allocation and distribution of sanctions.	A leader has command over different sanctions and related task records. These sanctions are essentially of informal nature.

- **Authority vs Leadership**

The authority exercised is a kind of legitimate power and people follow figures exercising it, because their positions demand so irrespective of the person holding the position. **Leaders in organizations and elsewhere may have formal authorities but they mostly rely on the informal authority that they exercise on people to influence them.** Leaders are trusted for their judgment and respected for their expertise, integrity etc and hence followed and not because they hold a certain position. For e.g. M.K. Gandhi for most part did not hold any official position to lead the Indian freedom struggle.

It is also important to understand that a formal authority and power emerging from it, might not always be able to influence people in the desired manner as; in times of crisis and difficulties people view it as coercion. On the other hand leadership tends to create followers out of free will and choice without forcing them to accept anything thrown their way. Authority rarely provides a scope for feedback, constructive criticism or opinions of the people on whom it is exercised however leaders provide ample platform to their followers to voice their thoughts and feedback.

When dealing with adults, the sole use of authority to direct and discipline them hardly works, leadership provides a better approach of sharing and involving thus building rapports with followers and creating long term relationships. Authority can hardly make people change their attitudes and behaviors with lasting effects and results however a leader inspires followers through self modeled ways and hence leadership displays greater effectiveness in addressing attitudes and behaviors of people.

Exercising authority sometimes limits the approaches to arrive at solutions for issues and problems while leadership encourages people to look beyond the obvious and think innovatively and sometimes emerge with radical solutions.

Apart from it, the biggest difference between the two as cited by Stephen R Covey is the moral authority held by leaders over the followers which is absent in the case of power from authority. Within the organizational setup when leaders also have moral authority on their subordinates by establishing a synchrony in their words and actions; the rest of the structure and processes of the organization also get aligned to it, thus creating a robust and transparent culture.

Authoritative way of working also encourages individuals to work in silos while in the organizations of today; the leaders need to have a complete picture and coordinate with other functions and departments as and when required. It is indeed difficult for mangers and leaders to move out of their circle of authority and coordinate and interact with external people. However the need of the hour and the more effective approach to leadership and management is when leaders come out of their comfort zone and move from exercising authority on a small group to leading the entire organization.

Individuals, who do not rely on authority but lead people, are the ones who enjoy the privilege of their ideologies and thoughts practiced by later generations long after they are gone. Even with individuals who held positions of responsibilities, the ones who actually led their people are the ones remembered and followed.

- **Leadership and Motivation**

    Motivation is a goal-oriented characteristic that helps a person achieve his objectives. It pushes an individual to work hard at achieving his or her goals. An executive must have the right leadership traits to influence motivation. However, there is no specific blueprint for motivation.

    As a leader, one should keep an open perspective on human nature. Knowing different needs of subordinates will certainly make the decision-making process easier.

    Both an employee as well as manager must possess leadership and motivational traits. An effective leader must have a thorough knowledge of motivational factors for others. He must understand the basic needs of employees, peers and his superiors. Leadership is used as a means of motivating others.

    Given below are important guidelines that outline the basic view of motivation:

    - Harmonize and match the subordinate needs with the organizational needs. As a leader, the executive must ensure that the business has the same morals and ethics that he seeks in his employees.

11

He should make sure that his subordinates are encouraged and trained in a manner that meets the needs of the business.

• Appreciation and rewards are key motivators that influence a person to achieve a desired goal. Rewarding good/ exceptional behavior with a small token of appreciation, certificate or letter can be a great motivator. If a certificate is awarded to a person, it should mention the particular act or the quality for which the individual is being rewarded.

• Being a role model is also a key motivator that influences people in reaching their goals. A leader should set a good example to ensure his people to grow and achieve their goals effectively.

• Encouraging individuals to get involved in planning and important issues resolution procedure not only motivates them, but also teaches the intricacies of these key decision-making factors. Moreover, it will help everyone to get better understanding of their role in the organization. The communication will be unambiguous and will certainly attract acknowledgement and appreciation from the leader.

• Developing moral and team spirit certainly has a key impact on the well-being of an organization. The metal or emotional state of a person constitutes his or her moral fabric. A leader's actions and decisions affect the morale of his subordinates. Hence, he should always be aware of his decisions and activities. Team spirit is the soul of the organization. The leader should always make sure his subordinates enjoy performing their duties as a team and make themselves a part of the organization's plans.

• A leader should step into the shoes of the subordinates and view things from subordinate's angle. He should empathize with them during difficult times. Empathizing with their personal problems makes them stronger-mentally and emotionally.

• A meaningful and challenging job accomplished inculcates a sense of achievement among employees. The executive must make their employees feel they are performing an important work that is necessary for the organization's well-being and success. This motivational aspect drives them to fulfill goals.

Remember, "**To become an efficient leader, you must be self-motivated**". You must know your identity, your needs and you must have a strong urge to do anything to achieve your goals. Once you are self-motivated, only then you can motivate others to achieve their goals and to harmonize their personal goals with the common goals of the organization.

- **Emotional Intelligence for Leaders**

An organization is made up of people and when people are involved, emotions automatically come into play, and a workplace is no different. It would be unwise to assume that a workplace is all objective, no-emotion only performance kind of a packed room where hormones have no scope to creep in however the fact is that emotions alone are the biggest motivator or de-motivator of an employee. The emotions alone, govern the performance and efficiency of a worker and had it not been the case, we would have never talked about the importance of work-life balance and for the present context, the need of emotionally intelligent leaders.

The current times are very dynamic not just economically but also socially where the social fabric is rapidly evolving due to globalization and other influences. The average age of the workforce is reducing and the leaders now look forward to managing people belonging to different cultures and backgrounds. In such a situation, it is important for a leader to be highly sensitized to the emotional aspects of his/her transactions with people. Emotional Intelligence is basically the ability to recognize and understand one's own feelings and emotions as well as those of others and use that information to manage emotions and relationships. The 4 important aspects of EI as proposed by Daniel Goleman are:

- Self Awareness
- Self Management
- Social Awareness
- Relationship Management or Social Skills

A leader tends to have a huge influence on the thoughts and motivation of people. He/she has the capacity to enthuse optimism and confidence in the followers and lead them to constructive endeavors which is called resonance and on the other hand they can negatively influence them to destruct, e.g of such leaders being Hitler and d Osama Bin Laden which is opposite to resonance called desonance.

Leaders are closely observed in terms of their body language, facial expressions etc. So, it is important for a leader to consider the non-verbal form of expressions as well, which may positively or negatively influence followers. Therefore, if a leader is talking about ethics in business with a slightly unconvinced and bemused look on his face, the followers make a note of it and the message is not received by them. A leader has to act as a role model too, supporting his statements, ideologies and values with appropriate actions.

As a leader one also has to be aware of one's own capabilities and weaknesses, it is difficult to accept guidance from a leader who is not self aware. As managers, leaders have to empathize as well with the situations, emotions, aspirations and motivations of the subordinates. A decreasing performance of a team member might be because of a number of reasons, a disruptive worker might be facing motivation issues and a subordinate who uses abusive language with others might be lacking confidence in his own abilities. A leader needs to discern facts and try and reach to deeper levels and understand things beyond obvious.

Apart from the above reasons, Emotional Intelligence is also important because the followers or subordinate expect it from their leaders. A subordinate working closely with the manager would expect the manager to understand his situation and priorities. And not surprisingly, whether manger does so or not, affects his level of commitment and performance at work. A leader has to suitably know and understand when he/she needs to be directive and when he needs to delegate. He/she needs to be aware, when the team members are acting as one unit and when there are differences.

It is sometimes awkward to address emotional aspects of transactions between people but leaders need to understand the importance and relevance of it as it has a huge impact on the performance outcomes. While conducting reviews and development dialogues, the feedback has to be delivered in a manner which is acceptable. The leader needs to be sensitive to the insecurities and apprehensions of the subordinates which sometimes might be expressed and sometimes kept undisclosed. At the senior level it is all the more

14

important as the senior executives find it hard to clearly outline their anxieties and differences and the leader has to anticipate some of them.

So, to be able to attract and retain talented subordinates and keep them motivated, a leader needs to brush up on his people skills and emotional intelligence, as all of them are not born with the charisma to hold people. Fortunately, emotional intelligence with practice and carefully directed efforts can be increased.

- **Organizational Leadership**

Organizations need strong leadership for optimum effectiveness. Leadership, as we know, is a trait which is both inbuilt and can be acquired also. **Organizational leadership** deals with both human psychology as well as expert tactics. Organizational leadership emphasizes on developing leadership skills and abilities that are relevant across the organizations. It means the potential of the individuals to face the hard times in the industry and still grow during those times. It clearly identifies and distinguishes the leaders from the managers. The leader should have potential to control the group of individuals.

An ideal organizational leader should not dominate over others. He should guide the individuals under him, give them a sense of direction to achieve organizational goals successfully and should act responsibly. He should be optimistic for sure. He should be empathetic and should understand the need of the group members. An organizational leader should not only lead others individually but also manage the actions of the group.

Individuals who are highly ambitious, have high energy level, an urge to lead, self-confidence, intelligence, have thorough knowledge of job, are honest and flexible are more likely to succeed as organizational leaders. Individuals who learn the organizational leadership develop abilities and skills of teamwork, effective communication, conflict resolution, and group problem solving techniques. Organizational leaders clearly communicate organizational mission, vision and policies; build employees morale, ensure efficient business operations; help employees grow professionally and contribute positively towards organizations mission.

- **Tips for Effective Organizational Leadership**

1. A leader must lead himself, only then he can lead others. He must be committed on personal and professional front, and must be responsible. He must be a role model for others and set an example for them.

2. A leader must boost up the morale of the employees. He should motivate them well so that they are committed to the organization. He should be well acquainted with them, have concern for them and encourage them to take initiatives. This will result in more efficient and effective employees and ensure organizational success.

3. A leader must work as a team. He should always support his team and respect them. He should not hurt any employee. A true leader should not be too bossy and should not consider him as the supreme authority. He should realize that he is part of the organization as a whole.

Organizational leadership involves all the processes and possible results that lead to development and achievement of organizational goals. It includes employees' involvement, genuineness, effective listening and strategic communication.

- **Leadership Ethics - Traits of an Ethical Leader**

Ethics refer to the desirable and appropriate values and morals according to an individual or the society at large. Ethics deal with the purity of individuals and their intentions. Ethics serve as guidelines for analyzing "what is good or bad" in a specific scenario. Correlating ethics with leadership, we find that ethics is all about the leader's identity and the leader's role.

Ethical theories on leadership talk about two main things: (a) The actions and behaviour of leaders; and (b) the personality and character of leaders. It is essential to note that "**Ethics are an essential to leadership**". A leader drives and influences the subordinates / followers to achieve a common goal, be it in case of team work, organizational quest, or any project. It is an ethical job of the leader to treat his subordinates with respect as each of them has unique personality. The ethical environment in an organization is built and developed by a leader as they have an influential role in the organization and due to the fact that leaders have an influence in developing the organizational values.

- **An effective and ethical leader has the following traits / characteristics:**

Dignity and respectfulness: He respects others. An ethical leader should not use his followers as a medium to achieve his personal goals. He should respect their feelings, decision and values. Respecting the followers implies listening effectively to them, being compassionate to them, as well as being liberal in hearing opposing viewpoints. In short, it implies treating the followers in a manner that authenticate their values and beliefs.

Serving others: He serves others. An ethical leader should place his follower's interests ahead of his interests. He should be humane. He must act in a manner that is always fruitful for his followers.

Justice: He is fair and just. An ethical leader must treat all his followers equally. There should be no personal bias. Wherever some followers are treated differently, the ground for differential treatment should be fair, clear, and built on morality.

Community building: He develops community. An ethical leader considers his own purpose as well as his followers' purpose, while making efforts to achieve the goals suitable to both of them. He is considerate to the community interests. He does not overlook the followers' intentions. He works harder for the community goals.

Honesty: He is loyal and honest. Honesty is essential to be an ethical and effective leader. Honest leaders can be always relied upon and depended upon. They always earn respect of their followers. An honest leader presents the fact and circumstances truly and completely, no matter how critical and harmful the fact may be. He does not misrepresent any fact.

It is essential to note that leadership is all about values, and it is impossible to be a leader if you lack the awareness and concern for your own personal values. Leadership has a moral and ethical aspect. These ethics define leadership. Leaders can use the above mentioned traits as yardsticks for influencing their own behaviour.

- **Leadership Strategy - Which Leadership Style to Follow ?**

Without an effective leadership strategy, it is believed, that the organizational strategies do not work. Best players in a team do not guarantee success without a great coach, similarly, work teams may not function effectively if leaders do not follow an appropriate leadership strategy.

To understand leadership styles here are three scenarios - *Scenario 1* - A Teacher gives a question to the class full of students, however, solves it for them; *Scenario 2* - A Teacher gives the question to the students and observes how students solve them; *Scenario 3* - A Teacher gives a question to the students and moves around the class, observes the students, and helps wherever required. Scenario 1 was "Leading from the Front", Scenario 2 was **"Supportive Leadership Style"**, and Scenario 3 was **"Interactive Leadership Style"**. Besides this the leadership styles / strategies could be based on personality traits like Directive Leadership, Structured Leadership, Intuitive Leadership, or Process Driven leadership.

- **Here are some tips while selecting leadership strategy / style:**

A leader must be aware of his / her personality traits and those of his team members / followers to understand which leadership style will be most effective.

A leader may not adopt a consistent leadership all through his / her career. Situational Leadership helps addressing varied needs / expectations of the followers as he the leader adopts a strategy based on a situation he / she is in. In case a leader has a self-reliant team, he needs to be using a directive leadership style or lead form the front. He could instead delegate and provide inputs where necessary.

18

A common mistake especially a lot of new leaders make is to copy established / well know leaders. Remember, each situation is unique and so are the followers. A leadership style which may be suited to a well known leader may not be appropriate for your team. Make no mistake here - do not try and imitate other leaders.

A leader will never be afraid of trying new approach to solve a work problem or address a conflicting situation. It is quite a possibility that a leader adopts a style that is not by the book.

A leader must keep enhancing his / her leadership skills. While on the job experience matters a lot, getting enrolled into leadership courses after detailed evaluation of the program and feedback of the participants will help implementing a leadership style more effectively.

It is often said that good leaders are born and not made; however, good leaders are those who are aware of their personality traits and also of their followers. They know which leadership style is to be adopted in a particular situation. Once this is done, there is a little challenge left for a leader to become a "good / great" leader.

- **Leadership Styles - Important Leadership Styles**

All leaders do not possess same attitude or same perspective. As discussed earlier, few leaders adopt the carrot approach and a few adopt the stick approach. Thus, all of the leaders do not get the things done in the same manner. Their style varies. The leadership style varies with the kind of people the leader interacts and deals with. A perfect/standard leadership style is one which assists a leader in getting the best out of the people who follow him.

Some of the important leadership styles are as follows:

Autocratic leadership style: In this style of leadership, a leader has complete command and hold over their employees/team. The team cannot put forward their views even if they are best for the team's or organizational interests. They cannot criticize or question the leader's way of getting things done. The leader himself gets the things done. The advantage of this style is that it leads to speedy decision-making and greater productivity under leader's supervision. Drawbacks of this leadership style are that it leads to greater employee absenteeism and turnover. This leadership style works only when the leader is the best in performing or when the job is monotonous, unskilled and routine in nature or where the project is short-term and risky.

The Laissez Faire Leadership Style: Here, the leader totally trusts their employees/team to perform the job themselves. He just concentrates on the intellectual/rational aspect of his work and does not focus on the management aspect of his work. The team/employees are welcomed to share their views and provide suggestions which are best for organizational interests. This leadership style works only when the employees are skilled, loyal, experienced and intellectual.

Democrative/Participative leadership style: The leaders invite and encourage the team members to play an important role in decision-making process, though the ultimate decision-making power rests with the leader. The leader guides the employees on what to perform and how to perform, while the employees communicate to the leader their experience and the suggestions if any. The advantages of this leadership style are that it leads to satisfied, motivated and more skilled employees. It leads to an optimistic work environment and also encourages creativity. This leadership style has the only drawback that it is time-consuming.

Bureaucratic leadership: Here the leaders strictly adhere to the organizational rules and policies. Also, they make sure that the employees/team also strictly follows the rules and procedures. Promotions take place on the basis of employees' ability to adhere to organizational rules. This leadership style gradually develops over time. This leadership style is more suitable when safe work conditions and quality are required. But this leadership style discourages creativity and does not make employees self-contented.

- **How to Create a Personal Leadership Brand ?**

Every leader has a personal leadership brand which might be carefully cultivated or intuitively perceived by leaders themselves and their followers. A personal leadership brand is an exclusive and a specific approach of a leader to address challenges and manage his/her transactions with their subordinates or followers. The best part of having a leadership brand is that it allows the flexibility to the leaders to define their own leadership objectives and then position themselves appropriately as per the need and situation. For example Lee Iacocca promulgated a leadership brand which was resolute, determined, persuasive and ready to take risks which helped him turn around Chrysler similarly Gandhi's leadership brand was that of integrity, honesty, principles, strength of character and above all truth.

It is essential for a leader to practice his/her leadership brand in thoughts and actions. How can a leader build up a leadership brand if they do not have one already. A leadership brand helps distinguish leaders and also outlines their approach, values, beliefs etc.

1. The first step definitely is identifying and establishing the results one wants to achieve by the end of a specific time period with a focus on preserving the interests of key stakeholders.

2. The second step becomes those distinguishing features with which one wants to be known as a leader. For e.g. one might identify drive for result as one's core strength area and can create a leadership brand based on the same

3. The next step becomes defining your identity. One might chose two or three word phrases to define their approach to leadership like Innovating to Excel etc

4. The last step becomes coming up with a leadership statement which conjuncts what one wants to be known for and what one wants to achieve

It is also important for leaders to check their leadership brand with seniors, subordinates and other stake-holders to understand their expectations from the role; and if any disconnect is pointed out, it needs to be incorporated.

Apart from the above aspects, leaders need to role model themselves and redefine their perceptions and ambitions to encompass the entire institution, which they represent. A leader needs to put the interests of the organization and stakeholders before his/her personal ambition and goals and strive to create success which is sustainable and does not need their constant presence.

21

The leaders need to understand that a personal leadership brand cannot be created overnight but credibility is earned the hard way, through years of perseverance. Once a leadership brand is created its acceptance and stability is established only after results are achieved. So, if a leader identifies certain goals but fails to achieve them, there are no takers for that leadership brand, similarly if a leader displays behaviors contradictory to what is outlined by his brand values, then also the credibility and respect of the brand is lost.

Level 5 Leadership

We have always associated leadership with a very visible and popular role which gives you recognition and a larger than life status as a leader however the level 5 leadership proposes quite opposing characteristics of a successful leader. Jim Collins and his research team were exploring the factors that made good companies great way back in the 1960s. It was then that they stumbled upon the Level 5 leaders who were invariably at the helm of affairs of all the companies which went on to become great in their respective fields. Who exactly is a Level 5 leader? Collins describes Level 5 leader as Humility + Will = Level 5. They are the nurturing leaders who do not want credit but want success to sustain over a longer period of time, long after they are gone.

Level 5 leaders are modest, shy and fearless and possess the capability to transform an organization from good to great without portraying themselves as wizards with magic wands. They prefer talking about the company and the contribution of other people but rarely about their role or achievements. Let us have a look at the hierarchical level of leadership identified:

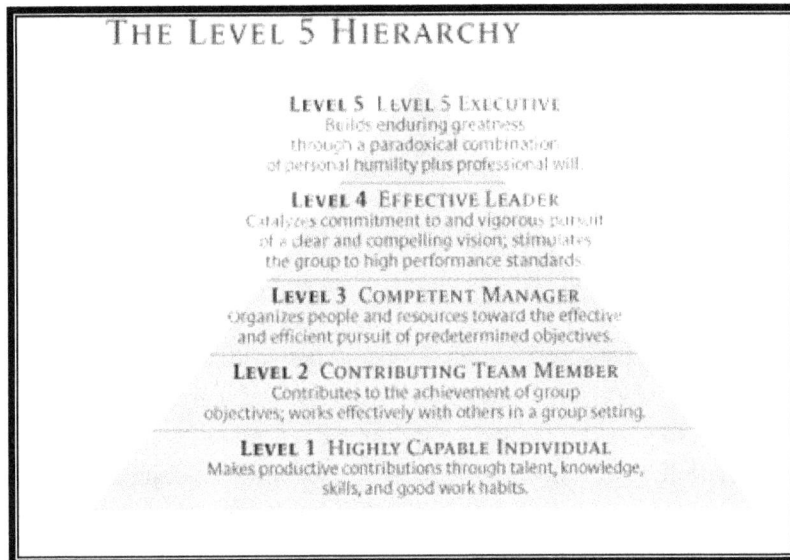

THE LEVEL 5 HIERARCHY

LEVEL 5 LEVEL 5 EXECUTIVE
Builds enduring greatness
through a paradoxical combination
of personal humility plus professional will.

LEVEL 4 EFFECTIVE LEADER
Catalyzes commitment to and vigorous pursuit
of a clear and compelling vision; stimulates
the group to high performance standards.

LEVEL 3 COMPETENT MANAGER
Organizes people and resources toward the effective
and efficient pursuit of predetermined objectives.

LEVEL 2 CONTRIBUTING TEAM MEMBER
Contributes to the achievement of group
objectives; works effectively with others in a group setting.

LEVEL 1 HIGHLY CAPABLE INDIVIDUAL
Makes productive contributions through talent, knowledge,
skills, and good work habits.

The Level 5 leadership clearly reestablishes the facts about a simply living and high thinking with an emphasis on personal humility taught by the older generations. The financial breakthroughs achieved by level 5 leaders prove that these characteristics can achieve tangible results as well. The most important example in this context can be cited of great world leaders like M.K. Gandhi and Abraham Lincoln, who always put their vision ahead of their egos. They came across as shy and defenseless people in their mannerism and speech but were hardly so when it came to actions. The other example from the business leaders who fitted perfectly into this category was Darwin E Smith who was the CEO of the paper company Kimberly-Clark and turned it around to become the biggest consumer paper product company. He was a unique mix of personal humility and will; combined with risk taking ability which made him a role model for the business leaders of today.

There are certain actions performed by Level 5 leaders which separate them from the rest of the leaders and senior executives.

▪ The first step if their ability to identify and include right people with them towards achieving goals. Unlike the traditional method of building strategies and then looking for the right people to carry them out, they take a different route. It's about getting the right people on board and then deciding on the destination.

■ They also do not shy away from facing and accepting brutal truths and realities of data, numbers and situations but at the same time they do not lose hope of a better future.

■ They also strive towards aligning consistent efforts towards a goal, rather than giving one massive push they believe in small but firm pushes to bring in the momentum.

■ They also exercise their judgment to understand an aspect, in depth and thoroughly, rather than burdening themselves with myriad information.

■ They practice and encourage a disciplined approach towards their work life and as visionaries use carefully identified technologies to give their businesses strategic advantage.

With the new concept of Level 5 leadership we come back to an age old question, can Level 5 leadership be learnt, if yes then how. According to Collins it is farfetched to suitably see whether it can be learnt or not but he surely identifies two categories of people, one who have the Level 5 Leadership in them, dormant, latent or unexpressed and others who do not have it.

So leaders who cannot look beyond their personal role, fame, achievements etc can hardly become Level 5 leaders. Only when they can put the larger good ahead of them, they transcend to the next level. This transition is not general but can be brought by some tragic accident, near death experiences or a life changing incident, as came across by Collins in his research. It would be appropriate to mention the name of M.K. Gandhi to understand it better. For Gandhi who had lived a comfortable life with a law degree from England had no experience of being oppressed by the ruling class until he was thrown out of a train despite carrying a first class ticket. His transition began from there, which later made him actively participate in the Indian Freedom Struggle.

Level 5 leadership is difficult to find and leaders who display it are a cut above the rest.

● **Situational Leadership - Meaning and Concept**

Leaders are essentially people who know their goals and have the power to influence the thoughts and actions of others to garner their support and cooperation to achieve these goals. In-case of leaders these goals are rarely personal and generally to serve the larger good. Ever since man was a hunter gatherer and lived in closely knit groups, they had leaders who led the hunting expeditions and took greater risk than the rest of the group members. In turn they were bestowed with larger share of hunting, respect and a higher position in the group. With changing times, how leadership is perceived has also changed, but, it remains an important aspect of social fabric nevertheless.

The initial theories proposed that leaders are born and cannot be created, there are certain distinct characteristics possessed by few men which make them leaders. [Read <u>Great Man Theory</u> and the <u>Trait Theory</u>]. However, for the current discussion we would try and take a closer look at another interesting theory which was proposed called Situational Leadership Theory. This theory says that the same leadership style cannot be practiced in all situations, depending upon the circumstance and environmental context the leadership style also changes. The pioneers of this theory were Kenneth Blanchard and Paul Hersey.

The model encourages the leaders to analyze a particular situation in depth and then lead in the most appropriate manner, suitable for that situation. The three aspects that need could be considered in a situation are:

- Employees' competences
- Maturity of the employees
- Complexity of the task
- Leadership style

In the Situational Leadership model, the leadership style has been divided into 4 types:

- **S1: Telling -** Telling style is associated with leaders who minutely supervise their followers, constantly instructing them about why, how and when of the tasks that need to be performed.

- **S2: Selling -** Selling style is when a leader provide controlled direction and is a little more open and allows two way communication between him/herself and the followers thus ensuring that the followers buy in the process and work towards the desired goals.

- **S3: Participating -** This style is characterized when the leaders seeks opinion and participation of the followers to establish how a task should be performed. The leader in this case tries creating relationship with the followers

- **S4: Delegating -** In this case, the leader plays a role in decisions that are taken but passes on or delegates the responsibilities of carrying out tasks to his followers. The leader however monitors and reviews the process.

It is also represented by a diagram most often which is below:

The developmental level of follower is an important indication for a leader to decide the most appropriate leadership style for them:

- **D4 - High Competence, High Commitment -** The followers who are identified in this category are the ones who have high competence and high commitment towards tasks to be performed. It might happen so that they turn out better than their leaders in performing these tasks. (For e.g. cricketing legend Sachin Tendulkar playing in the Indian cricket team under the captainship of Mahendra Singh Dhoni)

- **D3 - High Competence, Variable Commitment -** This category consists of followers who have the competence to do the job but their commitment level is inconsistent. They also tend to lack the confidence to go out and perform task alone. (E.g. President Barack Obama)

- **D2 - Some Competence, Low Commitment -** In this case, the followers have a certain level of competence which might be sufficient to do the job but they are low on commitment towards the tasks. Despite of having relevant skills to perform the task they seek external help when faced with new situations. (A team member made the trainer for new joiners)

- **D1 - Low Competence, High Commitment -** This category of followers may not have the specific skill required but they display a high level of commitment towards the task they have to perform, with confidence and motivation, they figure out ways to complete the tasks. (E.g. Mohandas Karamchand Gandhi, a lawyer by profession who spearheaded the Indian Freedom Struggle)

The above information regarding the style of leadership and the type of followers sure has a correlation to each other which forms the

26

basis of situational leadership. So, a situational leader would try to accommodate his leadership style as per the situation and the level of competence and commitment of his followers. This information is also an important aspect to consider when senior leaders act as coaches for their subordinates in the organizations.

Impact of Situational Leadership on Performance and Motivation

Leaders are role models who influence the culture, values, thoughts and actions of the organization and its people. The leadership style practiced by managers greatly influences the performance and productivity at the work place. The situation leadership model encourages managers to flexibly use their leadership style based on the situation and thus achieve effective results. Both at the middle managerial level where leaders work closely with people and at higher managerial level where leaders are responsible to a number of people, their approach has an impact on the motivational levels of the organization.

A leader needs to constantly inform him/herself of the motivational needs of the employees, one of simple factors of success cited in the organizations is a motivated workforce. The 4 leadership style of Telling, Selling, Participating and Delegating proposed in the situational leadership model can be used as per the motivational need of the subordinate. For example, for a senior manager who has been recently recruited and who boasts an illustrious career graph would need more responsibilities and opportunities to prove himself i.e. Delegating to remain motivated. On the other hand a fresher joining the organization may look at more Telling and a little participative approach to keep him/her motivated. A leader has to carefully evaluate and then decide on the right approach for the subordinate.

Situational Leadership has all the more relevance when teams work together especially across functions or locations. In these cases the team members might be physically separated from the leaders and the work situations might rapidly change, in such cases, maintaining the involvement and motivation level of team members becomes important. To create a high performance team that works effectively, the style that the leader would have to choose may be unique for each team.

Apart from this, a leader has to provide a vision to the people; it is the visions which help them direct and redirect their efforts towards it. In the recent times where changes are rapid in the organizations, the leaders have to be fully sensitized to what style would work the best, sometimes they might have to use a combination of styles to address issues effectively. For e.g. for a new change that is being introduced, the initial approach has to be Selling, where people are educated about the change, the next step becomes Telling, where the people have to be instructed as to how the change would be carried out. When the change starts settling in and people adopt it, they style can become Participating, where the people get an opportunity to partner in the change and take it ahead. The last change would then become delegating when the change can now be carried on by the others. The ultimate aim of any leader is to smoothly arrive at a stage where he/she can easily delegate tasks without worrying about its completion or effectiveness.

The leadership style also has a bearing when leaders are to act as mentors and coaches for their subordinates. The learning style of the subordinates can be interpreted in the terms of Telling, Selling, Participating and Delegating. Some subordinates learn when they know exactly what is to be done, some learn when they know the importance of the task, some learn when they understand the how of what is to be done, and ultimately some learn when they are actually allowed to perform the task. When a leader acts as a coach he/she has to keep in mind what works best for the coachee and the fact that what works for one might not work for the other.

- **Influence of Situational Leadership Styles on Subordinate Development**

As we know that the situational leadership theory proposes that a leader needs to change his/her leadership style as per the situation and environment. Leaders also need to consider the level of their followers; to decide on a particular leadership style. Let us now try to explore, whether the leadership style practiced by the leader influences the subordinates at all and if they do then how does it happen?

In the organizational context a manager is not just a superior for his team of subordinates but is also their leader. This implies that as a manager he/she has to make sure that the subordinates are working cohesively as a unit to achieve department or function goals, and if a problem arises the manager has to step up and take the responsibility as a leader.

How would a manager ensure that each member and the team collectively are working towards that common goal? Sometimes, the contribution from each member is not equal, some are working and some are not, which often leads to imbalances and negativities in the team and work environment.

It is the leadership style practiced by the manager which to quite an extent is responsible for such a situation to arise. Every team has people who have different level of competence and commitment towards the work they do, some are pro-active and others need to be pushed. In either case, the role of the manager as a leader becomes all the more important where he/she needs to be flexible with the kind of leadership style they can practice with each subordinate.

Let's try to understand the relationship between leadership styles and subordinate development in a little detail. Recall the four situational leadership styles identified by Hersey and Blanchard. They were:

- Telling
- Selling
- Participating
- Delegating

Now, have a look at the following diagram which depicts the development level of the followers based on their competence and commitment towards their work.

So, which leadership style would be appropriate with each of these levels? A manager as a leader has to partner in the developmental journey of his/her subordinate. For a subordinate who is at a level D1, where he has low competence but high motivation, the leadership style could be Participative where the leader involves the subordinate and further motivates him to build on his competence to increase his/her effectiveness at tasks.

For a subordinate, who stands at a level D2 where he has some competence but lacks or shows inconsistent commitment, the leader can resort to the Telling style. In this case, the subordinate cannot be relied upon to complete the task without instructions and guidance. For the subordinates who fall into the category of D3 or high competence but variable commitment, the leadership style could be Selling as the leader would have to create a buy in from these subordinates to secure their commitment towards the task. Since they have the necessary competence to do the task, instructions are not required but such subordinates wish to see the value of the work they are doing to get committed to it.

And lastly, if the subordinate fall into the category of D4 where they have both high commitment and high motivation, the leadership style best suited could be Delegating, where the leaders need to understand, acknowledge and appreciate the competence and commitment of the subordinates and entrust them with responsibilities.

Leaders have to be aware of their surroundings and sensitized to the abilities and motivations of their followers/subordinates in order to be able to take effective decisions.

- **Introduction to Leadership Development**

Leadership development entails nurturing, encouraging, incubating, and mentoring prospective leaders. In many organizations, the HR department in conjunction with senior management identifies potential leaders or fast trackers who are capable and ensures that they are motivated and encouraged to give their best. This form of mentoring and coaching of future leaders happens through organizational commitment to their development that includes sending them to specialized training programs, making them attend targeted workshops, and taking them to resorts and getaways with the express purpose of ensuring that these prospective leaders get all the encouragement and strategies to groom them into senior level positions.

It needs to be remembered that leadership development is not only about the organizational need for grooming prospective leaders but also to do with the candidates themselves showing the inclination and the aptitude to be groomed as leaders.

30

The point here is that **leadership development is a two-way process that is symbiotic with both the organization and the candidate showing interest in mutual success**. Only when both sides are keen on helping each other grow can true organizational development take place. This is the case with organizations like Infosys, Sony, and IBM, Fidelity etc where potential leaders are identified early on in their careers and given the necessary backing for them to blossom as true leaders. It needs to be mentioned that leadership in the current turbulent business landscape is a combination of traits and vision and hence potential leaders ought to have that rare combination of business acumen and risk taking along with visionary ideas with integrity. Integrity has been mentioned along with the rest as the financial crisis of 2008 proved that business leaders without integrity are a burden to the organization. Hence, these traits should be spotted and then adequate environmental support given so that leaders are groomed appropriately.

Leadership development is as much about traits as it is with experience and this is where the role of the mentors appears. Existing senior management leaders can help potential leaders perform better and give them tips and insights into how the business world operates so that they have an idea about how they have to respond to tricky and thorny issues. The point about real world experience is that many potential leaders might have the necessary traits and ambition but lack the insights into what makes for a successful leader in the real world. This is where the experience of the senior leaders in organizations helps as they can provide valuable guidance to the potential leaders on how to address tricky real world problems.

Finally, **leadership development entails commitment, patience, and skill and unless the potential leaders are committed to stay with the organization for an extended period, there is no point in grooming them**. Though many organizations have moved away from making the employees sign bonds, they still groom only those employees who have been with them for a while and who, in their estimation, are going to stick with the company for a longer term.

- ### Leadership: Intrinsic v/s Extrinsic Motivation

The steps that organizations can take to ensure that leaders are groomed by identifying potential leaders and then fast tracking them. This is looks at one trait of potential leaders that goes a long way in determining the success or otherwise of the leaders. This trait is motivation, the will to succeed, and the desire to do well, which is an integral part of leadership development. **Motivation is necessary for leaders to reach the top and the types of motivation are intrinsic and extrinsic motivation.** Intrinsic motivation is the will to succeed by changing oneself from within and extrinsic motivation is the performance that is driven by external rewards. The point here is that individuals have to be motivated from within and then they have to be rewarded with external benefits and benefits to achieve the best results in organizations.

This is clear from the emphasis that HR managers and senior executives place on matching rewards with performance that is first driven from within. To explain further, leaders have to be motivated to perform by a strong urge to succeed from within and then the external rewards have to match their performance.

Employees who are only motivated by external rewards do not make great leaders and conversely, employees who are not rewarded for their performance stagnate and lose morale. Hence, the strategic fit between intrinsic motivation and extrinsic motivation has to be just right for organizations to get the best from their employees. This is the reason many organizations go the whole distance in aligning incentives with performance. Unless employees are motivated from within, incentives and rewards can only help that much and unless high performers are rewarded appropriately, intrinsic motivation withers away.

The recent global economic crisis brought to the fore the system of flawed incentives that was in place in the investment banks and Wall Street firms. The point here is that though the bankers were performing well, the rewards were too high and this made them take unnecessary risks and not heed to the "inner voice" that guides us all in our daily life and career. Since this internal director compels us to be ethical and normative, the absence of conscience among the bankers led to their taking unnecessary risks with their business practices. The underlying incentives that were disproportionate to their actual performance made them oblivious to risk and ethics. Hence, the balance of intrinsic and extrinsic motivation has to be just right for high performance that is also ethical and normative in nature.

Finally, all of us need a higher vision for ourselves to succeed and this is the extra something that drives us to greater heights. As many theorists have pointed out, once the need for wealth and status is achieved, the higher needs of self-actualization or the need to be driven by vision appears. Hence, the conclusion is that intrinsic motivation is the driver for success as leaders and the rewards have to match this but not exceed beyond a certain point.

- **Appointing Home Grown Leaders to the Top Posts versus Bringing in Leaders from Outside**

One of the thorny issues facing senior management in many organizations is the debate over grooming leaders from within and then appointing them to the top posts versus brining in leaders from outside and then making them the CEO. The debate is not confined to a particular country and occupies the energies of corporate leaders worldwide. This is because many organizations prefer that they have people at the helm who have come up the ranks as opposed to having outsiders take to the top slot. The issue is contentious because **appointing outsiders to the top slot evokes antipathy from those who have been overlooked and hence can lead to unnecessary tensions and lack of cooperation**.

The way out for many boards of corporations is to conduct a search process wherein they consider both the homegrown talent as well as outsiders and decide purely based on merit and nothing else.

However, this is easier said than done since **appointing homegrown talent has its advantages**. First, these leaders know the organizational intricacies like the back of their hand and hence can be expected to bring familiarity and a sense of purpose to managing the organization given their knowledge of the bureaucracy and contacts. The point here is that since homegrown talent already knows the ropes of the organizational ladders, they are able to translate this advantage into actionable results. Further, they also have allegiance to power centers within the organizations and hence, this gives them an edge over outsiders, as they are able to navigate the treacherous waters of the organizational politics. However, this can also turn into a disadvantage as they would be beholden to certain power centers and hence would biased towards them and this leads to exacerbation of existing divisions.

On the other hand, **bringing in outsiders makes sense when the organization is in crisis and needs a fresh perspective**. The CEO drawn from the wider corporate world can start afresh without any leftover baggage and can ensure that he or she brings a new set of lens with which the organization can determine its vision. This is the case that works best when corporates are floundering because of intra organizational rivalries and hence bringing in outsiders would be a good idea to rejuvenate the organization. However, this is also easier said than done since there is a possibility of all factions ganging up on the new CEO and denying him or her chance to rebuild the organization.

The best possible course would be to have leaders groomed before the person at the top retires and hence, ensure that these leaders step into the shoes of the retiring leader. However, as the case of the Infosys leadership transition proves, grooming leaders from within can also spark a boardroom war. Ultimately, the solution to this tricky issue needs to be found by recourse to a mixture of firmness and astuteness and there are no easy answers to the question as to whether homegrown leaders make the best choice or outsiders are the preferred alternative.

- **Transformational Leadership and its Value in the Corporate World**

Transformational leadership is one of the many kinds of leadership that is usually on display in the real world. The reason for focusing on this particular type of leadership is to highlight the need for transformational leadership in these tough times when the ability to articulate a vision and motivate the employees along with putting the company before self is badly needed.

The point here is that unless corporate leaders display transformational leadership in these turbulent times, the organizations that they head would not be able to withstand the headwinds of turbulence and navigate the choppy seas of competition. Examples of transformational leaders include the late legendary Steve Jobs of Apple, Bill Gates of Microsoft, Jack Welch of GE, and NR Narayana Murthy of Infosys. Along with these figures, the names of Aditya Birla and Ratan Tata come to mind when listing the hall of fame for transformational leaders.

Transformational leadership goes beyond normal leadership and as the name implies, it results in a complete rejuvenation of the company and a transformation of its place in the corporate world. For instance, the late Steve Jobs succeeded in altering consumer perceptions of computing, mobile technology, and the way in which media is consumed in the digital age. Similarly, Bill Gates can be credited with pioneering the personal computing revolution that has benefited Billions of people around the world and has transformed the landscape of the business world. Further, NR Narayana Murthy can be said to have incubated a whole industry with his stewardship of Infosys that resulted in the IT sector in India taking off in a big way and emerging as a force to reckon with in the world. Finally, Ratan Tata and Aditya Birla can be credited with transforming what were essentially family owned businesses into a new look professionally managed conglomerates that redefined the map of the corporate world in the county and abroad.

Moreover, these figures succeeded in not only driving their companies to greater heights but also ensured that they were trailblazing and path breaking in their endeavors. For instance, Ratan Tata introduced the concept of the one Lakh Car in India, which ensured that millions of middle class consumers could convert their dream of owning a car into reality. Apart from Ratan Tata, Capt. Gopinath of the erstwhile Deccan Airways fame transformed the concept of aviation in India by providing the common person with the wherewithal and the connectivity needed by introducing the concept of SimplyFly or bringing flying to the masses.

We shall be discussing each of these figures and the traits of transformational leadership in other as well. It would suffice here to state that what each of these leaders had in common was a vision and the ability to translate it into actionable results and actualize it in practice.

The point to be noted is that many leaders have the vision but fail to translate into reality. While some leaders (who are truly extraordinary) like the Late Legendary Dhirubhai Ambani had a combination of vision, mission, ambition, and hard work, which proved that he remains a towering figure in the list of transformational leaders.

- **Leadership for the 21st Century**

The previous one discussed the importance of transformational leadership in the corporate world. This is looks at the traits and attributes needed in the 21st century business landscape. Though on transformative leadership touched upon several aspects of leadership in the contemporary times, this is expands on it by including the role of ethics and value based leadership for the 21st century.

If there is one lesson to be learnt from the ongoing global financial crisis, it is that the business leaders failed miserably to implement value based systems and instead, gave free rein to greed and the pursuit of monetary rewards at the expense of everything else. Indeed, as the behavior of the bankers and the financial elite proved in the aftermath of the crisis, they were more interested in furthering their goals rather than thinking about the welfare of the people.

The business landscape of the 21st century is extremely competitive and this uber connected world means that leaders have extraordinary demands placed upon them. However, this does not mean that they take shortcuts to success and sacrifice ethics and principles at the altar of profits.

Instead, what is needed in the current times is that leaders must not only be transformative but also practice value-based leadership that gives importance to ethics and humanitarian principles. As the various points on corporate social responsibility discussed, we can navigate this century only if we cooperate along with compete and only if we share along with earn. Hence, the solution to the crisis facing humanity is clear: we are all in the same boat and hence we sink or swim together. This is the place where leaders can display their leadership skills and ensure that they lead by example and not rock the boat and instead, teach others to steer it to safety.

Further, **leaders in the 21st century have another vital function i.e. they have to be the ideal role models for the coming generation** and since anyone who has grown up over the last two decades would testify, they have been influenced by leaders from all occupations. For instance, it is common for people in their thirties now to admire and idolize business leaders like Steve Jobs, Bill Gates, Jack Welch, and NR Narayana Murthy. In the same way, the upcoming generation needs to have the current leaders of the business world as role models and hence a holistic approach that does not put profits before people all the time, that does not place undue emphasis on making money as the sole aim, and finally, the transformative power of business to solve social problems with the leaders taking the lead, are traits and attributes that are needed from the leaders of the 21st century.

In this context, it is worth mentioning that the present generation is very cynical and disinterested in the leaders of the present because of the lack of these motivating characteristics from the leaders. Indeed, this is something that is food for thought for the present day leaders and something that they should actualize in practice.

- **The Transleader: Strategy, Leadership, and the Soul**

One of the big ideas being bandied about in recent times is the interaction of strategy, leadership, and the soul of organizations which when they work in tandem can create exceptional leaders in the 21st century business landscape. This is the premise of the book by Sertl and Huberman who have theorized that for leaders to be successful in the 21st century, they need a blend of strategy that is rethought every now and then, leadership that is dependent on sensing relevance in all areas of life and business, and finally, the integration of the values and inner beliefs of the individual with that of the organization. The point here is that for leaders to succeed in the 21st century landscape, an integrated model of leadership is what is needed and which Sertl and Huberman propose.

To take the first aspect, **strategy in this model of leadership is ever changing to reflect the fluid marketplace** where a rapid turnover of ideas, fads, and trends means that strategy has to be continuously refined and rethought.

Strategy in this case is not merely something that is drawn up every few years and then followed irrespective of the changes in the external world. Instead, strategy changes with each relevant change of the trends. Note the emphasis on the term relevant as strategy cannot change with each passing fad or trend and instead, the leader must evaluate the relevance of the trend to his or her business and then strategize accordingly. Moreover, there needs to be a dynamic strategy in place to tackle any tectonic shifts in the business world and hence strategy must not be static.

Next, **leadership ought to be responsive to complexity, ambiguity, and uncertainty**. There is no point for a leader to be smug in the confidence that he or she knows every detail of the business and hence does not see the need for working through these aspects. Further, the days of leadership based on knowledge and experience is outdated, as the "transleader" needs to be transformational in the sense that he or she should combine knowledge and experience along with an intuitive understanding of the three aspects listed above. The point here is that the Transleader must be able to intuit and sense the changes in the external world and react and respond accordingly.

The third aspect, which is revolutionary, is that **the Transleader must be someone whose inner values and beliefs mirror that of the organization and vice versa**. Only through this integration would the organization's power and efficiency would be leveraged and the leader and the employees can find success and fulfillment in their careers. The point here is that the alignment of this "soul" across the customers, employees, and business partners is a fundamental necessity for the success of the leader and the organization. In conclusion, the organizations of the future would have transleaders who can play a transformative role and by reenergizing the soul of the organizations, they can lead them to greater successes.

- **Three Traits of Effective Leadership**

We have introduced the concept of Transleader in the previous points. We discussed how a leader who is integral to the organization and vice versa could prove to be an effective leader. Taking the discussion forward, in this reviews the three traits that make for effective leadership and separates leaders from followers. The three traits that are discussed here are character, vision, and relationship effectiveness. It needs to be mentioned that these three are not the only traits but more like these traits are essential to leadership. In other words, these traits are necessary but not exhaustive.

To take the first trait, **character of the leaders is important as it defines who they are, what they will do, and what they would not do, and what they stand for**. In other words, the individuals who have their values and beliefs in deep-rooted ways would be able to withstand the pressures and tests of their values and principles. Since leadership is all about being the final decision maker, it is important for the leaders to be committed to principle and be driven by values instead of merely pursuing the bottom line. Hence, the first trait of effective leadership is the strength of character that leaders have.

The next trait of effective leadership is the ability to be a visionary and have a sense of future possibilities. The point here is that leaders are individuals whom the followers look up to guide them towards the future and hence leaders ought to have visionary capabilities to actualize this need. We have examples from business, government, and society where true leaders like the late legendary Steve Jobs, Bill Gates, and Larry Paige and Sergei Brian of Google proved that they had game changing ideas about the future. The essence of 21st century leadership is not only about peering into the future but also making the future a place for the organization to thrive and succeed. In other words, leaders are those individuals who are not threatened by the future and instead like the legendary mythological prophets in every religion can show pathways to the future which the followers can follow.

The third trait is how effective the leaders are in personal relationships. Since most leaders realize that, the whole game of life is all about people and the relationships that one builds with those whom one encounters; effectiveness in personal relationships distinguishes the true leaders from the rest. Though this does not mean that leaders need only charisma or be a people's person, the point here is that by nurturing and incubating relationships, the leaders can prove that their behavior towards others and the effectiveness, which they display in their relationships, pervades the whole organization and infects others positively to do the same.

Finally, it needs to be noted that leaders must find the organizations that they are comfortable in and hence their characteristics and the organizational DNA must be aligned to create a winning combination. After all, one can be the right person for the wrong job and the wrong person for the right job and what matters is whether one is the right person for the right job.

- **Reinventing Management for the 21st Century**
  A Failure of Leadership in Management ?

The world is facing unprecedented upheaval and chaos in virtually every sphere of human activity. Where it is economic crisis, climate change, resource depletion, failure of political systems, or the breakdown of the social order, there is only gloom and doom all over us. Hence, **the broader question is whether we have had a failure of leadership in the sense that there are no leaders in business or society who are able to show the way and lead us from the front.**

The narrower question is why did management thought that was responsible for so many achievements and improvements in material prosperity over the last century or so fail us so miserably. It is these questions that explore to illuminate how a new generation of leaders in business and society emerge and provide us with exemplary leadership that would be known for decades.

Some Trends and how they are going to shape the future

First, the Millennial Generation or those born in the period 1980-1995 have come of age at a time when the world is in crisis. As discussed above, the problems are many but the options are limited. With social, economic, and political transformation, the present generation can again rejuvenate the world of business and chart a new course for humanity. Since this generation came of age when the internet was making its presence felt and are now experiencing the mobile wave, it is safe to say that the emerging generation would have the necessary knowledge and

40

experience in the technologies of the future to make a difference to the world of business. The other trend is that though people are living and working longer, they no longer are loyal to a single organization and instead, are only loyal to their professional identities. For instance, while the norm in the earlier generations was to stick to a job throughout ones working life, now it is considered something of an aberration if people do not change jobs.

- **Need to Reinvent Leadership and Management**

These trends discussed above have led to a fundamental change in the economic logic of the firm. If the earlier management thought was about capital as the scarce resource and the strategic imperative of the firm was to transform inputs into outputs in an efficient manner, now knowledge is the scarce resource and firms succeed not only because of the efficiencies of their processes but also because of creativity and innovation. Hence, these aspects have led to a basic change in the way management and leadership is understood and therefore, there is a compelling case to be made to reinvent management.

Closing Thoughts

Finally, we discussed the positive aspects (reinventing leadership) and the negative aspects (the gloomy situation, as it exists now). For all future leaders, there is a message here: which aspect you chose to be the basis of your worldview would depend on your attitude and your approach to life. If you think that the future is all gloomy, then no amount of persuasion is going to make you change your mind. On the other hand, if you think that the future holds promise, then you can start thinking seriously, about how you can revitalize the field of business and management. The choice is yours.

- **Six Essential Social Media Skills that Every Leader Should Have**

The social media revolution has taken the business world by storm. Few areas of business and society have been left untouched by the social media revolution. Concomitant with this trend, companies and business leaders have realized the immense power of social media and have started to tune their strategies accordingly. **This discusses six essential social media skills that every leader must have to succeed in the world of Web 2.0**

1.   Becoming a Producer

Business leaders must incorporate social media in their communications by producing and sharing rich media in their blogs and by opening Facebook and Twitter accounts through which they can communicate to their stakeholders. Of course, this is easier said than done as most business leaders are behind the curve where social media is concerned. To alleviate this shortcoming, business leaders have to learn to use technology more effectively and more efficiently. This means that they would have to upgrade their technical skills and become social media savvy. This literacy and expertise in using social media would be a major advantage to them as they go about communicating to their stakeholders.

2.   Becoming a Distributor

The convergence of vertical broadcast media and horizontal participatory media means that the business leaders must master the knowledge of this interplay between these very different paradigms at work. For instance, traditional communication is largely hierarchical and follows command and control flow. On the other hand, social media follows system dynamics that determine whether the content goes viral or not and hence, business leaders must become experts in controlling the distribution of content that would let them influence the flow of communication throughout the organization. Knowing what to say and how to say are as important as the distribution of these messages to the wider audience.

3.   Becoming a Recipient

A common refrain one hears in the information age is that we are besieged with information overload. Drowning in a never reducing flood of Facebook posts, tweets, and emails, business leaders can get lost in this electronic maze that would impair their ability to sift through the content and determine what is useful or not. Given the fact that traditionally business leaders have had assistants to wade through the information and give them what is necessary, they might have to employ web savvy staff to do this for them in the changing world of web 2.0

42

4.   Becoming an Advisor and Orchestrator

Once the business leaders realize the importance of web 2.0 for their organizations, the next task is to ensure that they let this insight percolate throughout the organization. In other words, they have to become change agents wherein they would harvest the potential of social media by inspiring their employees to embrace social media effectively and efficiently. To do this, they must have the skills described in the three sections above and on top of that, they must don the hat of evangelicals who trumpet the advantages of social media to their employees.

5.   Becoming an Architect

The social media revolution has challenged the traditional conceptions of organizational communication, as there is a thin line between free exchange of information throughout the organization and the risk of irresponsible use that poses existential threats to the organizations. For instance, it is common in many firms to ban the use of social media by the employee during the time they spend in office. Instead of these autarkic responses, business leaders must develop appropriate strategies that would merge vertical accountability with horizontal collaboration. In other words, the merger of organizational hierarchical communication with that of informal networks of communication is the challenge before business leaders.

6.   Becoming an Analyst

Finally, business leaders must not only leverage social media for their organizational success but also be ahead of the curve by riding the wave of change and anticipating the next paradigm shift. As the next generation internet of things is already on the horizon, business leaders must use all their intellect and experience to see how their organizations can profit from the coming changes. This means wearing multiple hats at once and ensuring that they are ahead of the curve instead of behind it.

- **Social Stratification and Hierarchy: What Business Leaders Ought to Know**

Rise above Social Stratification

All societies are stratified and have elements of hierarchy amongst their members. If the notion of Varna or Caste is prevalent in the East, then the notion of class and race is prevalent in the west. In recent decades, with the advent of modernity and postmodernism, there has been a tendency among social scientists to dismiss the concept of stratification and insist that societies become egalitarian. Without getting into the merits and demerits of particular types of social stratification, it is important to remember that in all societies, the coalescing of people around specific identities forms the glue that binds them together and in turn gives coherence and sense of purpose to society. Of course, this is not to say that without racial or ethnic identities, societies would flounder. Indeed, with modern notions, the concept of these groupings has become antiquated. The point that is being made here is that in the absence of formalized structures and institutions that promote equality, the ethnic and the racial groupings provide their members with a sense of security and a fallback option in hard times. Indeed, the success of the East in recent times has been attributed to the prevalence of family values, group identity, and the networks of racial and ethnic groups that provide the much-needed support for starting new ventures or growth of existing ones. On the other hand, the widening income inequality in the West, which is another form of stratification, has been blamed for the deterioration and degeneration in those countries.

- **Hierarchy and its uses and disadvantages**

Turning to the concept of hierarchy, it is indeed the case that any organization or grouping of people has to be hierarchical if decision-making and responsibility as well as accountability of these groupings is to actualize. In other words, though most of us hate the fact that hierarchy among peoples make some superior and others inferior, for purposes of cohesion and coherence as well as discipline and order, some semblance of control should be present which is provided by hierarchy. As mentioned earlier, this is not a justification for the prevalence of group identities based on narrow conceptions of human nature. Rather, the examination of what are trends in societies is the focus and as empirical research shows, these groupings are very much present both in the West (based on income and class along with race) as well as in the

East (based on ethnic, religious, and other social groupings). Hence, any policymaker or business leader has to necessarily take into account these realities and without paying too much importance to the divisions, has to work with them and within them as well as rise above them if he or she has to make an impact on the organizations that they head.

- **Be Global in Attitude yet Local in Execution**

The concepts of stratification and hierarchy are closely intertwined, as one cannot exist without the other. Though this is reprehensible fact that some groups are deemed superior to others, the fact that business leaders ought to understand the different social structures and base their strategies on shrewd observation cannot be denied. As has been emphasized throughout this, the best approach would be one where hierarchy is determined based on merit and stratification is absent except where the need for decision-making and execution of strategy is concerned. in other words, the truly great business leaders are aware of the societal differences but rise above them and ensure that their strategies are realistic without getting caught in the inter group and intra group warfare and strife.

Closing Thoughts

Finally, it is high time we acknowledge the fact that the 21st century belongs to global leaders who realize the importance of cosmopolitan leadership rather than antiquated divisions. On the other hand, they need to be cognizant of the local realities which would make them avoid the mistake of forcing global notions on the society without a clear understanding of the on the ground situation.

- **Leadership in the Face of Adversity**

The best leaders are those who can face adversity and turnaround their companies from times of trouble to positions of strength. Throughout history, the leaders who were feted and achieved fame are those who took charge during times of crisis and managed to actualize victory. Similarly, in recent decades, the business world has seen a surfeit of leaders who stepped in when their companies were going through a rough patch and with their leadership ensured that they could revive and rejuvenate their companies. For instance, the legendary Lee Iacocca who was at the helm in Ford Motors took over the leadership of another auto major, Chrysler when the company was going through troubled times and in a matter of a few years ensured that it turned the corner. The case of the late Steve Jobs is another example of how he was recalled to Apple when the company was facing adversity and shrinking market share and with his game changing approach to business ensured that Apple is the most profitable company in the world. In recent weeks, the respected founder of Infosys, NR Narayana Murthy, has been recalled from retirement and tasked with the job of restoring the company to its previous dominant position.

The Elements of Leadership in Adversity

What these examples tell us is that true leadership is a phenomenon that thrives on challenges and the authentic leaders are those who can turn adversity into opportunity. These leaders follow the maxim that when the going gets tough, the tough get going. More often than not, they lead by example and from the front, which means that they set a benchmark for the employees to follow which often motivates the employees to perform better and actualize their potential. In many cases, leadership in times of adversity works by rejuvenating the company through stirring words and actions and the latter are more important as the nuts and bolts of leadership lies in execution. The example of how Ratan Tata turned the TATA group around is a case in point as to how leaders need to work more and talk less and ensure that execution is as important as or more important than planning and conceptualization. When one considers businesses that are moribund or near to failure, we find that bringing in leaders who can inspire and actualize success helps a lot in reviving the fortunes of these companies. For instance, the example of how the public sector enterprises in India have been made profitable and that too worthy of high market capitalization from a situation where they were close to being shut tells us that collective leadership in the face of adversity is as important as charismatic and visionary leadership.

The Characteristics of Leadership in Adversity

The key point to be noted here is that anyone can ride the success of companies but it takes a real leader with vision, mission, and hard work to turn around companies that are struggling. One of the important aspects of such leadership is that they must have a team of peers and managers who are as committed to the revival of the company as the leader. This is critical and necessary for leaders tor turnaround the companies. Another aspect about such leadership is that they must be given time to succeed as transformations do not happen overnight unless one expects miracles, which is something most business leaders discount. Therefore, time, patience, effort, and cooperation are all factors that play a crucial role in determining whether the leader succeeds in his or her mission. The case of the former Defense Secretaries, Robert McNamara in the 1960s, and Robert Gates in recent years illustrates that for deep changes to actualize; the leaders need time, patience, and energy as well as a single-minded devotion to their tasks.

- **Leadership Theories - Important Theories of Leadership**

Just as management knowledge is supported by various theories, the leadership function of management too is authenticated by various theories. While the behavioural theories of leadership focused on discovering the constant relationship between leadership behaviours and the group performance, the contemporary theories emphasized the significance of situational factors (such as stress level, job structure, leader's intelligence, followers' traits, etc.) as well.

Some of the **important leadership theories** are as follows:
- Blake and Mouton's Managerial Grid
- House's Path Goal Theory
- Great Man Theory
- Trait Theory
- Leadership-Member Exchange (LMX) Theory

- Transformational Leadership
- Transactional Leadership
- Continuum of Leadership Behaviour
- Likert's Management System
- Hersey Blanchard Model
- Fiedler's Contingency Model

- **Transformational Leadership Theory**

Creating high-performance workforce has become increasingly important and to do so business leaders must be able to inspire organizational members to go beyond their task requirements. As a result, new concepts of leadership have emerged - transformational leadership being one of them.

Transformational leadership may be found at all levels of the organization: teams, departments, divisions, and organization as a whole. Such leaders are visionary, inspiring, daring, risk-takers, and thoughtful thinkers. They have a charismatic appeal. But charisma alone is insufficient for changing the way an organization operates. For bringing major changes, transformational leaders must exhibit the following four factors:

- **Model of Transformational Leadership**

Inspirational Motivation: The foundation of transformational leadership is the promotion of consistent vision, mission, and a set of values to the members. Their vision is so compelling that they know what they want from every interaction. Transformational leaders guide followers by providing them with a sense of meaning and challenge. They work enthusiastically and optimistically to foster the spirit of teamwork and commitment.

Intellectual Stimulation: Such leaders encourage their followers to be innovative and creative. They encourage new ideas from their followers and never criticize them publicly for the mistakes committed by them. The leaders focus on the "what" in problems and do not focus on the blaming part of it. They have no hesitation in discarding an old practice set by them if it is found ineffective.

Idealized Influence: They believe in the philosophy that a leader can influence followers only when he practices what he preaches. The leaders act as role models that followers seek to emulate. Such leaders always win the trust and respect of their followers through their action. They typically place their followers needs over their own, sacrifice their personal gains for them, ad demonstrate high standards of ethical conduct. The use of power by such leaders is aimed at influencing them to strive for the common goals of the organization.

Individualized Consideration: Leaders act as mentors to their followers and reward them for creativity and innovation. The followers are treated differently according to their talents and knowledge. They are empowered to make decisions and are always provided with the needed support to implement their decisions.

The common examples of transformational leaders are Mahatma Gandhi and Obama.

Criticisms of Transformational Leadership Theory

- Transformational leadership makes use of impression management and therefore lends itself to amoral self promotion by leaders

- The theory is very difficult to e trained or taught because it is a combination of many leadership theories.

- Followers might be manipulated by leaders and there are chances that they lose more than they gain.

Implications of Transformational Leadership Theory

The current environment characterized by uncertainty, global turbulence, and organizational instability calls for transformational leadership to prevail at all levels of the organization. The followers of such leaders demonstrate high levels of job satisfaction and organizational commitment, and engage in organizational citizenship behaviors. With such a devoted workforce, it will definitely be useful to consider making efforts towards developing ways of transforming organization through leadership.

- **Transactional Leadership Theory**

The transactional style of leadership was first described by Max Weber in 1947 and then by Bernard Bass in 1981. This style is most often used by the managers. It focuses on the basic management process of controlling, organizing, and short-term planning. The famous examples of leaders who have used transactional technique include McCarthy and de Gaulle.

Transactional leadership involves motivating and directing followers primarily through appealing to their own self-interest. The power of transactional leaders comes from their formal authority and responsibility in the organization. The main goal of the follower is to obey the instructions of the leader. The style can also be mentioned as a 'telling style'.

The leader believes in motivating through a system of rewards and punishment. If a subordinate does what is desired, a reward will follow, and if he does not go as per the wishes of the leader, a punishment will follow. Here, the exchange between leader and follower takes place to achieve routine performance goals.

These exchanges involve four dimensions:

Contingent Rewards: Transactional leaders link the goal to rewards, clarify expectations, provide necessary resources, set mutually agreed upon goals, and provide various kinds of rewards for successful performance. They set SMART (specific, measurable, attainable, realistic, and timely) goals for their subordinates.

Active Management by Exception: Transactional leaders actively monitor the work of their subordinates, watch for deviations from rules and standards and taking corrective action to prevent mistakes.

Passive Management by Exception: Transactional leaders intervene only when standards are not met or when the performance is not as per the expectations. They may even use punishment as a response to unacceptable performance.

Laissez-faire: The leader provides an environment where the subordinates get many opportunities to make decisions. The leader himself abdicates responsibilities and avoids making decisions and therefore the group often lacks direction.

Assumptions of Transactional Theory
- Employees are motivated by reward and punishment.
- The subordinates have to obey the orders of the superior.
- The subordinates are not self-motivated. They have to be closely monitored and controlled to get the work done from them.

Implications of Transactional Theory

The transactional leaders overemphasize detailed and short-term goals, and standard rules and procedures. They do not make an effort to enhance followers' creativity and generation of new ideas. This kind of a leadership style may work well where the organizational problems are simple and clearly defined. Such leaders tend to not reward or ignore ideas that do not fit with existing plans and goals.

The transactional leaders are found to be quite effective in guiding efficiency decisions which are aimed at cutting costs and improving productivity. The transactional leaders tend to be highly directive and action oriented and their relationship with the followers tends to be transitory and not based on emotional bonds.

The theory assumes that subordinates can be motivated by simple rewards. The only 'transaction' between the leader and the followers is the money which the followers receive for their compliance and effort.

- **Difference between Transactional and Transformational Leaders**

Transactional leadership	Transformational Leadership
Leadership is responsive	Leadership is proactive
Works within the organizational culture	Work to change the organizational culture by implementing new ideas
Transactional leaders make employees achieve organizational objectives	Transformational leaders motivate and empower employees to achieve company's objectives by appealing to

through rewards and punishment	higher ideals and moral values
Motivates followers by appealing to their own self-interest	Motivates followers by encouraging them to transcend their own interests for those of the group or unit

Conclusion

The transactional style of leadership is viewed as insufficient, but not bad, in developing the maximum leadership potential. It forms as the basis for more mature interactions but care should be taken by leaders not to practice it exclusively, otherwise it will lead to the creation of an environment permeated by position, power, perks, and politics.

Continuum of Leadership Behaviour

The leadership continuum was originally written in 1958 by Tannenbaum and Schmidt and was later updated in the year 1973. Their work suggests a continuum of possible leadership behavior available to a manager and along which many leadership styles may be placed. The continuum presents a range of action related to the degree of authority used by the manager and to the area of freedom available to non-managers in arriving at decisions. A broad range of leadership styles have been depicted on the continuum between two extremes of autocratic and free rein (See figure 1). The left side shows a style where control is maintained by a manager and the right side shows the release of control. However, neither extreme is absolute and authority and freedom are never without their limitations.

The Tannenbaum and Schmidt continuum can be related to McGregor's supposition of Theory X and Theory Y. Boss-centered leadership is towards theory X and subordinate-centered leadership is towards theory Y.

A manager is characterized according to degree of control that is maintained by him. According to this approach, four main styles of leadership have been identified:

- **Tells:** The manager identifies a problem, chooses a decision, and announces this to subordinates. The subordinates are not a party to the decision making process and the manager expects them to implement his decisions as soon as possible.

Figure 1: Continuum Leadership Behaviuor.

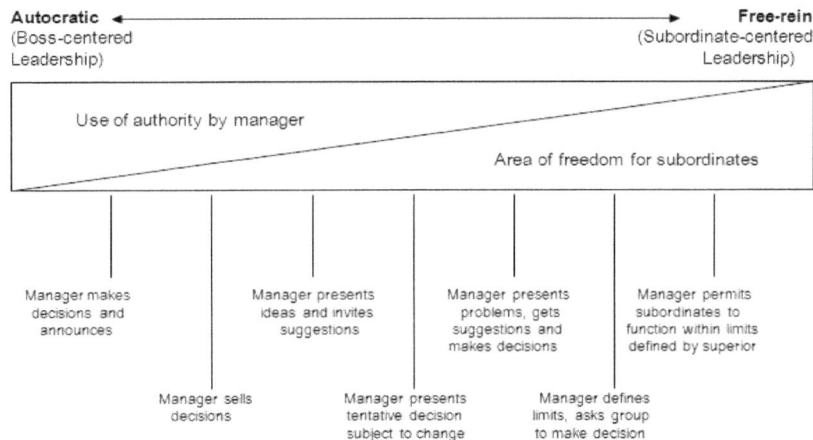

- **Sells:** The decision is chosen by the manager only but he understands that there will be some amount of resistance from those faced with the decision and therefore makes efforts to persuade them to accept it.

- **Consults:** Though the problem is identified by the manager, he does not take a final decision. The problem is presented to the subordinates and the solutions are suggested by the subordinates.

- **Joins:** The manager defines the limits within which the decision can be taken by the subordinates and then makes the final decision along with the subordinates.

According to Tannenbaum and Schmidt, if one has to make a choice of the leadership style which is practicable and desirable, then his answer will depend upon the following three factors:

- *Forces in the Manager:* The behavior of the leader is influenced by his personality, background, knowledge, and experience. These forces include:

    i.   Value systems
    ii.   Confidence in subordinates
    iii.   Leadership inclinations
    iv.   Feelings of security in an uncertain situation

- *Forces in the subordinate:* The personality of the subordinates and their expectations from the leader influences their behavior. The factors include:

    i.   Readiness to assume responsibility in decision-making
    ii.   Degree of tolerance for ambiguity
    iii. Interest in the problem and feelings as to its importance
    iv.   Strength of the needs for independence
    v.   Knowledge and experience to deal with the problem
    vi.   Understanding and identification with the goals of the organization

If these factors are on a positive side, then more freedom can be allowed to the subordinate by the leader.

- *Forces in the situation:* The environmental and general situations also affect the leader's behavior. These include factors like:

    i.   Type of organization
    ii.   Group effectiveness
    iii. Nature of the problem
    iv.   Time pressure

When the authors updated their work in1973, they suggested a new continuum of patterns of leadership behavior. In this, the total area of freedom shared between managers and non-managers is redefined constantly by interactions between them and the environmental forces. This pattern was, however, more complex in comparison to the previous one.

Conclusion

According to Tannenbaum and Schmidt, successful leaders know which behavior is the most appropriate at a particular time. They shape their behavior after a careful analysis of self, their subordinates, organization, and environmental factors.

Likert's Management System

Rensis Likert and his associates studied the patterns and styles of managers for three decades at the University of Michigan, USA, and identified a four-fold model of management systems. The model was developed on the basis of a questionnaire administered to managers in over 200 organizations and research into the performance characteristics of different types of organizations. The four systems of management

54

system or the four leadership styles identified by Likert are:

- **System 1 - Exploitative Authoritative:** Responsibility lies in the hands of the people at the upper echelons of the hierarchy. The superior has no trust and confidence in subordinates. The decisions are imposed on subordinates and they do not feel free at all to discuss things about the job with their superior. The teamwork or communication is very little and the motivation is based on threats.

- **System 2 - Benevolent Authoritative:** The responsibility lies at the managerial levels but not at the lower levels of the organizational hierarchy. The superior has condescending confidence and trust in subordinates (master-servant relationship). Here again, the subordinates do not feel free to discuss things about the job with their superior. The teamwork or communication is very little and motivation is based on a system of rewards.

- **System 3 - Consultative:** Responsibility is spread widely through the organizational hierarchy. The superior has substantial but not complete confidence in subordinates. Some amount of discussion about job related things takes place between the superior and subordinates. There is a fair amount of teamwork, and communication takes place vertically and horizontally. The motivation is based on rewards and involvement in the job.

- **System 4 - Participative:** Responsibility for achieving the organizational goals is widespread throughout the organizational hierarchy. There is a high level of confidence that the superior has in his subordinates. There is a high level of teamwork, communication, and participation.

The nature of these four management systems has been described by Likert through a profile of organizational characteristics. In this profile, the four management systems have been compared with one another on the basis of certain organizational variables which are:

- Leadership processes
- Motivational forces
- Communication process
- Interaction-influence process
- Decision-making process
- Goal-setting or ordering

55

- Control processes

On the basis of this profile, Likert administered a questionnaire to several employees belonging to different organizations and from different managerial positions (both line and staff). His studies confirmed that the departments or units employing management practices within Systems 1 and 2 were the lease productive, and the departments or units employing management practices within Systems 3 and 4 were the most productive.

Advantages

With the help of the profile developed by Likert, it became possible to quantify the results of the work done in the field of group dynamics. Likert theory also facilitated the measurement of the "soft" areas of management, such as trust and communication.

Conclusion

According to Rensis Likert, the nearer the behavioral characteristics of an organization approach System 4 (Participative), the more likely this will lead to long-term improvementin staff turnover and high productivity, low scrap, low costs, and high earnings.if an organization wants to achieve optimum effectiveness, then the ideal system

- **Leadership and Trust**

Trust seems to be the key trait linked with leadership. A leader cannot lead if his followers do not trust him. A leader discovers the employees'/followers problems and tries to solve them, but it is the trust that his followers hold on him which tells whether the leaders retrieve the knowledge and intellectuality required to solve the problems. Trust can be defined as an optimistic belief that others will not perform (via words, acts, or final conclusions) in an opportunistic manner.

For trust to nurture, an appropriate atmosphere is needed. This responsibility rests with the leader in an organization. The employees will show absolute trust in the leaders when they observe ideal/excellent character in them. **Leaders play a crucial role in developing and maintaining trust of organizational employees**. Reliability, empathy and realization of individual/personal goals assist the leaders to gain trust of the employees/followers. When the employees show trust in a leader, they are ready to be exposed to the actions of the leader- self-assured that their interests and rights will not be harmed.

The primary facets of trust are:
- Truth/Honesty
- Proficiency/Competency
- Commitment
- Reliability
- Sincerity/Openness

A leader should keep his followers informed, be fair and objective, share his feelings, be honest, allow the followers to constantly direct their decisions, maintain their promises, and earn respect of the followers. All this will contribute in building trust upon the leaders.

A trust-centred leadership will offset worries, apprehensions, and low-morale by developing a trustworthy environment where employees feel secure, confident and keyed up. The employees will be ready to take initiative, give suggestions, share their views, feel unhesitant to take risk and will contribute completely in such an atmosphere of trust.

Due to instability and unpredictability of organizations today, building of trust between managers as leaders and their employees is essentially required.

- **How to be a Good Leader - What makes Leadership Effective ?**

Leadership is a significant aspect of management. In order to ensure organizational success, co-operation from subordinates as well as greater efficiency, it is important for a manager to be a great, effective and a true leader. An effective and true leader is one who does not put himself before others. He is very humble, deferential and altruistic.

The required aspects of effective leadership are as follows:
- Motivation
- Commitment
- Self-sacrifice
- Honesty
- Determination

- Resourcefulness
- Daring
- Knowledge
- Good communication skills
- Passion
- Responsibility
- Judgement

Leadership is boosting an individual's performance to a greater benchmark, the developing of an individual's personality crossing its standard boundaries. It is a combo of mindframes, traits, skills, and knowledge. Leadership means adhering to the following principles:

- Respect your followers.
- Acknowledge the followers efforts if there is success, and do not blame them for any failure.
- Encourage participation of all in decision-making.
- Make the goals clear to all.
- Support the followers in accomplishing the objectives and in reaching their potential.
- Discover efficient and economical ways of performing the task.
- Ensure proper and <u>effective communication</u> with the followers. There should be no place for misunderstanding and misinterpretations.
- Be a trainer and not an opponent/critic.

An effective leader is one who meets the job requirements, team requirements as well as individual requirements. While concentrating on the job, a leader would synchronize the departmental goals with the organizational goals. He would ensure that the employees have the required skills and competencies for performing the job effectively and efficiently. He would provide the employees the essential resources for performing the job such as time, knowledge and equipment. He would ensure that employees have no difficulty in performing the tasks assigned to them. And finally, an effective leader would review progress and give the employees a feedback of their performance.

When a leader is focusing on people, he must be compassionate and empathic. He should listen to the employees with understanding. He must respect their views and ideas. He must train and coach them and make an effort to eliminate unnecessary obstacles from the employees' work responsibilities.

Finally, when an effective leader focuses on team, he should coordinate team's efforts. He must celebrate team's success. He should review and promote friendly and social environment. He should develop a team spirit and achievement sense among the employees as a team.

- **Effective Leadership Skills - What it takes to be an Effective Leader**

Who is a leader - A strong leader is one who thinks and plans ahead. He is ready with solutions and he understands the pulse of his employees. However, what are the skills which a leader must possess to be able to do his job well?

Read on to know how even YOU can be an effective leader...

Master Your Time: Effective leaders will always be in a position to manage their time well. They would know how to prioritize list of activities / pending tasks. Most important - they would know the different between 'urgent' and 'important'. Remember, not everything that is urgent is important. Also, not everything that is important is urgent.

Ask Questions: Leaders will ask questions that help them assess employees' contribution to the organization and also help employees understand how better they can contribute towards organizational goals. A Leader must ask his / her employees - the task they perform, do they feel their task is linked to the big picture, and is there anything that comes in the way of their performance.

Provide Work-Life Balance: In today's world where working hours are on a rise, an effective leader must ensure that his / her workers are able to maintain a balance between their personal and professional lives. Effective leaders should always lead by example by leaving on time, avoiding meetings during Fridays or end of the business days, not calling employees on their day off. Remember, an effective leader will have effective followers only if they are not burnt out or feel they are over worked.

Manage Employee's Professional growth: An effective leader will always chart out a personal development plan [PDP] along with his / her employee. He would identify the training the employee will need to go through keeping in mind his personal development plan. The employees will feel encouraged and valued.

Let your employees speak: An effective leader has to be a good listener. Have an "open hour" with your employees and let them speak their heart out. You will be surprised to know the number of ideas they have. Always follow and believe in the mantra "Silence is Golden". Your employees will feel they are being heard and they also have a way to express their thoughts.

Facilitate Brainstorming... Generate ideas: Effective leaders will always encourage people to get together in a room and brainstorm on ideas to solve a particular problem. Remember, discussions are always healthy and almost all the times they also help creating solutions which are mutually agreed upon.

Create Talent Pool: Smart leaders will always be ready for any shortage in staff. They will have their talent pool ready in case of any crisis situation. They will ensure that every employee has a trained / trainable back-up.

Be Courageous: As per Peter Drucker, "whenever you see a successful business, someone once made a courageous decision". An effective leader will always be ready to take difficult / courageous decisions when required.

Be Competent: The art of "tooting your own horn without blowing it" is a delicate balance of demonstrating your "expertise" and "taking credit" in a way that people notice their success. And one of the safest ways to do it is to celebrate and bring attention to team achievements. Praise people for good work, and when you do so, be specific on what exactly you liked. Shaking hands is a gesture that will show them that you are actually happy about their contribution and their success. And thus, you will prove out your competence as a leader.

Be Visionary: What's lying ahead in future is a topic of fascination and has mystic charm. This is a trait of absolute confidence and should be handled with care. It is important to make goals specific, with possible outcomes and benefits, without making promises that you may not be able to keep. A successful leader knows his goals and checks if performance and goals are in symmetry.

- **Leadership Vision**

True leaders have a vision, that is, they have a potential to view the present as it is and to invent a future culminating out of the present. A leader with a vision can foresee the future and can remain in the present. A vision is an end towards which leader can spend and direct his energy and resources. Leaders share a dream and a path which the employees want to share and follow. Leadership vision is not restricted to organizational written mission statement and vision statement. It is well demonstrated in the actions, beliefs and values of organizational leaders.

"If there is no vision, people cannot survive." This is applicable both in business as well in life. Leaders who lack vision cannot succeed in life and they work in a standard and monotonous manner. Vision is not a fantasy for leaders; rather it is a truth that has yet to come into practice. So as to achieve vision, a leader must exert special extra efforts and have robust confidence and devotion to realize the vision. Vision acts as an internal force propelling a leader to act. It provides a leader an objective. The consistent existence of a vision makes a leader progressive despite various hardships and obstacles. Vision is a bond that unites the individuals into team with a mutual goal.

Recognition of a leader's vision by the organizational employees is very essential as it makes the employees well aware of what the organization is trying to achieve. Vision has the strength to move the employees out of monotonous work life and to place them into a new challenging and dynamic work. Vision must be:

- Rational
- Reasonable
- Innovative
- Credible
- Clear
- Motivating and stimulating
- Challenging
- Reflective of organizational beliefs, values and culture
- Concrete

It is a leader who moulds, interprets, communicates and represents the vision. Vision is a portrait and depiction of what a leader aspires his organization to be in long-term.

- **Different Types of Power**

Power has been an important aspect of human civilization since time immemorial. Power might be physical, political or social. In the context of business as well, power dynamics tend to influence decisions and people transactions heavily. So defining power can be difficult as it is understood and interpreted in several ways however power can definitely not be called a force which gets you what you want. Power basically emanates from position or authority which can influence people both positively and negatively.

For simplicity and understanding purposes power is usually classified into following categories:

1. **Coercive Power-** This kind of power involves the usage of threat to make people do what one desires. In the organizational set up, it translates into threatening someone with transfer, firing, demotions etc. it basically forces people to submit to one's demand for the fear of losing something.

2. **Reward Power-** As the name suggests, this type of power uses rewards, perks, new projects or training opportunities, better roles and monetary benefits to influence people. However an interesting aspect of this type of power is that, it is not powerful enough in itself, as decisions related to rewards do not rest solely with the person promising them, because in organizations, a lot of other people come into play like senior managers and board.

3. **Legitimate Power-** This power emanates from an official position held by someone, be it in an organization, beurocracy or government etc. The duration of this power is short lived as a person can use it only till the time he/she holds that position, as well as, the scope of the power is small as it is strictly defined by the position held.

4. **Expert Power-** This is a personal kind of power which owes its genesis to the skills and expertise possessed by an individual, which is of higher quality and not easily available. In such a situation, the person can exercise the power of knowledge to influence people.

Since, it is very person specific and skills can be enhanced with time; it has more credibility and respect.

5.   **Referent Power-** This is a power wielded by celebrities and film stars as they have huge following amongst masses who like them, identify with them and follow them. Hence, they exert lasting influence on a large number of people for a large number of decisions; like from what car to buy to which candidate to choose for a higher office in the country.

So, power can be defined in a number of ways however what is important is the usage of the power by people who possess it. Within the organizational context the power dynamics and equations need to be carefully managed as they have a huge impact on the motivation and engagement level of employees. It also defines the organization's culture in general and people transactions within the organization in particular. A very hierarchy and power driven organization finds it difficult to accommodate new and innovative ideas, any change is vehemently refused, egos clash and lesser opportunities are made available for the high performers, thus delaying organizational growth. On the other hand, in an organization which is flat in structure, people are encouraged to innovate and explore, thus bringing in new concepts and ideas to accelerate organizational growth and expansion.

- **Women and Leadership**

Unlike male leaders, the reference point for a good leadership has been inadequately defined for women leaders. The traditional and concretely defined gender roles in the society have also influenced the research and findings on women leadership, a role, which is divorced from the stereotype roles identified for women. So, it becomes rather challenging for a woman to first reach a position of leadership and then struggle for acceptance and credibility as a leader. It is ironic that in both conservative and liberal cultures, the presence of women in positions of influence, power and leadership is far less than desirable. However, with changing times and workforce trends, this is also changing and more and more women are breaking the glass ceiling to actually lead.

It would be interesting to explore certain aspects of leadership in the context of women, do the same principles of leadership apply for both genders or there is something like feminist leadership which exclusively outlines the desirable behaviors from women leaders.

Let us try to explore the context of women leadership in an organization. Traditionally women had hardly been in senior positions within organizations to exercise power and authority. This meant that when they actually got a chance to do so, they had to live up to the expectations of a male leader, which involved being authoritarian, directive and masculine at times. However, researches conducted show that women in leadership positions believe in more participative and collaborative approach which involves, working with people rather than making people work. Women are also good transformational leaders than men and use the nurturing, caring and engaging approach towards subordinates.

However, it is never easy for a women leader to get accepted by male subordinates, in the bargain they end up compromising on their leadership behaviors to make them more acceptable and less intimidating for the male subordinates. This leaves a very narrow scope of what is acceptable and what is not from a female leader. For example, an aggressive and direct behavior from a male leader is appreciated but a similar approach from a woman leader is termed as unnecessarily dominating. Similarly, if the woman leader displays the feminine behavior of nurturing and care, they are looked upon as lacking firmness and assertiveness.

However there are certain clear benefits of a women leader as well, what a male leader needs to learn through deliberate efforts comes naturally to woman leaders like Emotional Intelligence, coaching and mentoring instincts, collaboration and participation etc. since, women leaders can collaborate effectively, they face relatively lesser challenges in managing teams separated by function and location. With their high emotional intelligence, they also understand the motivational factors of subordinates better and can also manage appropriately their diverse culture and backgrounds.

The women leaders face greater and bigger challenges than male leaders as they also have to battle against perceptions. With more women taking up leadership roles, the hitherto unknown issues and challenges of a leadership position are now beginning to surface. The increasing stress level and dual responsibility of work and home with the constant pressure of proving herself, makes life difficult for them. However with a more sensitized organization and support extended by family, women leaders are also proving themselves as able and competent visionaries for e.g. the recent appointment of Virginia M Rometty as CEO and President of IBM Corporation. With such decisions of appointing women at critically and strategically important positions reaffirm the fact that women leaders are as good as a male leader. The evaluation of leadership effectiveness is only fare when it is based on leadership style and results achieved rather than on gender.

- ### What are the Challenges in Leadership ?

Being a leader is not quite a cakewalk. Infact, to be very honest; managing people is one of the most challenging tasks. You really need to extract the best out of your team members and handhold them even in the worst situations. We all want to lead a team, but have we ever realized what are the challenges faced by a leader? Remember, a leader is just like the captain of a ship. One wrong decision and the entire blame comes on you.

The biggest challenge in leadership is to listen to everyone's opinions and come to a mutually beneficial solution. You just can't afford to ignore anyone, else he/she would turn out to be your biggest enemy and would neither respect you nor bother to listen to you. Agreed, there are all types of people around. You may like someone; you may not like someone at the workplace, but that does not mean that you start being rude to the person you are not comfortable with. Avoid favouritism. As a leader; you really need to be impartial towards everyone. Not every individual has the quality of being fair towards people. As humans, we generally tend to develop feelings of jealousy and hatred towards people we do not like. Remember, such negative feelings have no place in the professional world. Sit with your subordinates, listen to their grievances and always try to come up with innovative solutions. Never ever loose your temper. The moment you do so, trust me, very soon your name would appear in the bad books of employees.

A leader has to win the trust of his/her subordinates. And that is again a big challenge. Yes, you would be surprised to see that the colleague who used to call you his best friend has all of a sudden started avoiding you and is actually jealous of your promotion and has problem with you being his team leader. A leader, most importantly has to understand the psychology of individuals. Never feel bad about the sudden change in the behaviour of your colleagues. Try to keep yourself in their shoes. Do not start showing your bossy attitude. Sit with your subordinates and make them realize that your job is not to rule over them but work as a team. Making people work together is a big challenge in itself. Remember, any problem in the team, you will be held responsible. In case of misunderstandings and conflicts, intervene immediately. Listen to both the parties and resolve the problem at the earliest.

As a leader, you are the face of your team. A team manger ought to act as a bridge between the employees and the management. It is your responsibility to ensure your subordinates are happy with their work, their bills are being released on time and they are overall satisfied with their jobs. There are several external challenges as well in leadership. Lack of projects, scarcity of funds and lack of support from clients are some of the external challenges faced by a leader. Your subordinates will come to you for work and it is your duty to delegate responsibilities. If your team members are unable to bring work from clients, immediately take the charge. If there is a financial crunch and your subordinates are not getting salaries on time, you just can't afford to take the back seat. Emergency situations are unpredictable. A leader needs to stand by his team members at the times of crisis. You just can't run away from the situation. Remember, a boss is always referred to as a Hitler, no matter how much he thinks for his team. A boss - employee relationship is more of a hate than a love relationship. Make your subordinates feel comfortable. Do not force them to call you "Sir". Respect is always commanded and never demanded. You need to inspire your team members for them to look up to you and treat you as their mentor.

- **Tips to Overcome Challenges in Leadership**

Leadership indeed becomes a challenging job, if managers do not understand their employees well. You can't make employees work by scolding or being rude to them. Bosses are successful only when their employees look up to them and treat them as their role models.

Let us go through some tips to overcome challenges in leadership:

A leader needs to inspire his/her subordinates. Don't expect your juniors to concentrate on work if you yourself are not serious about your work. The best tip to overcome challenges in leadership is to understand the psychology of your subordinates. An individual who is leading a team of say five employees also has a reporting boss. Now try to analyze your relationship with your reporting authority. How would you feel if your superior insults you in front of all? Yes, you would never like to see your Boss's face again and he/she would become your biggest enemy. Yes, your team members also go through the same feeling when you do not scold them in private. Always keep yourself in other's shoes before reacting. Yes, a boss needs to be a little strict, else no one would actually listen to him/her but that does not mean you really need to be a Hitler. A Hitler like Boss finds it extremely challenging to make his team work and deliver.

The next tip to overcome challenges in leadership is to encourage open communication among team members. You are sadly mistaken if you feel that your job as a team manager is to sit in your closed cabin and sleep. A leader needs to know what his team members are up to but yes there is a difference between knowing and interfering. You need to give your team members the space they require. The best way to win the trust of your team members is to sit with them once in every week and enquire whether they are happy with their current role or not? Remember, employees who are not satisfied with their jobs are the ones who create problems and badmouth their organization. Let them come up with their grievances and it is your duty to provide the most appropriate solution as soon as possible. Trust me, if minor issues are addressed at the earliest, you would never have a problem later on. Communicate in the presence of all. Common policies ought to be discussed in the presence of all so that information reaches in its desired form.

As a leader, you need to have the quality of extracting the best out of your team members. Remember, a leader ought to lead from the front. Set an example for your subordinates. Make them work as a single unit. Once in a while go out with them for sales meetings, client presentations, and so on. You need to assure your employees that you are always there with them, even in the most critical times. A boss needs to protect his team. Handhold and guide them as to what is right and what is wrong? Employees tend to blindly follow their leaders, thus as Bosses, you need to watch your behaviour carefully. Encourage ice breaking activities at the workplace. Celebrating festivals together, going out for lunches and team outings once in a while go a long way in strengthening the bond among employees and their superiors.

Top performers need to be appreciated. Do not be rude to the ones who have not performed well this time. It would demotivate them. Sit with them and try to work on their problem areas. Trust me, this way, your subordinates would not only become your biggest fan but also strive hard to perform better.

Planning intelligently also goes a long way in overcoming challenges in leadership. Do not depend on a single plan. It is always better to be ready with Plan B than to crib later.

Leadership is no rocket science. You just need to treat your subordinates with utmost respect and care.

- **Role of Communication in Overcoming Leadership Challenges**

  Communication plays a crucial role in not only overcoming challenges in leadership but also strengthening the bond among employees. Bosses need to communicate with their subordinates and guide them whenever required. It is essential for the team managers to remain in constant touch with their team members.

  What are the common problems faced by team leaders ?

  - Employees do not listen to them.
  - Bosses are not aware as to what their employees are up to ?

- Employees do not achieve targets within the stipulated time frame.
- Employees do not respect them and often lie and bunk office.

The solution to all the above problem lies in effective communication. Being a boss does not mean that you have to adopt a Hitler like attitude and be very strict with your subordinates.

As a boss, you do not have to scare them but make them work as a single unit. **Remember, half of the problems disappear when discussed**. You just need to sit together, talk, sort out differences and reach to solutions which would not only benefit the organization but also your team. Most of the times, we take every initiative to solve a problem except discussing the same amongst ourselves. The moment we start talking amongst ourselves, we realize that half of the solution is with us only. Team leaders need to motivate their subordinates to sit together, discuss issues face to face and sort out things among themselves.

Remember, any minor issue left unattended leads to major problems later on. If you feel any of your team members is not doing justice at work, you have all the rights to discuss with the individual concerned. Simply showing employees the exit door is not the ideal solution. After all how many employees you would terminate? At the end of the day, you need people to work and deliver. Even the most stubborn employee would start listening to you, if you sit with him in private and address his grievances. Initiate the concept of weekly meetings where all employees can come together on a common platform to share their experiences, brainstorm and contribute in strategies and policies. Employees seldom share their problems with their superiors. It is the team leader's duty to sit with his team, find out their strengths and weaknesses and work on their problem areas. Remember, that you are being appointed as a team manager because your organization feels that you are capable of making your team work. **You can extract the best out of your team members only when you communicate with them on a regular basis**. Yes, conversation over the phone and email not always help. Meeting face to face is also important as it gives employees the confidence that their boss is always by their side even during the most crucial times.

You need to make your team feel special for them to develop a feeling of attachment not only with their team but also with the organization. Wish them on their birthdays, anniversaries or any other important occasion. Trust me, they would start respecting you more if you send them a nice birthday card or for that matter congratulate them on their achievements. Never forget to appreciate them, if they have performed well. This would not only motivate them to perform even better next time but also encourage others to pull up their socks and work harder to set new benchmarks.

Discuss with your team members before reaching to any concrete strategy for the team. Every employee needs to have a say in major decisions. Let employees talk, share their experiences, discuss work and also gain from each other's knowledge.

Communication is an effective tool which would not only make you a popular and favourite boss in the organization but also motivate your team members to love, care and support you unconditionally.

- **Role of Management/Organization in Overcoming Leadership Challenges**

It is rightly said that if you get a good boss, you are the luckiest employee and if your boss does not support you, God can only save you! Leaders are appointed to provide a direction to the team members and also motivate them to deliver their level best. Is there any employee who admits that he does not work hard in office? Infact no one. Then why do you think very few people really make it big and get the opportunity of managing individuals? Remember, being a leader is not everyone's cup of tea.

Management plays an essential role in not only recruiting the right person as a team leader but also overcoming the challenges faced in leadership. Management needs to understand the importance of a leader. Do we need a boss just for the sake of it? Do not ask the wrong person to manage a team. This would not only demotivate the other individuals but also spoil the office environment. It is the responsibility of the human resource department and of course the top management to ensure that the right person gets the opportunity to lead a team. If you are hiring an individual from outside, make sure you do check his credibility, past achievements, experience, educational qualification and most importantly his/her background before rolling out the appointment letter.

Disaster is bound to happen if a person with no experience or for that matter a criminal background is hired as a team leader. Neither your employees would respect such a person nor bother to listen him/her. No matter of strictness, team meetings, stringent policies would help if the responsibility of managing people is on the shoulders of a wrong person. Management needs to be extra careful in situations where existing employees are being promoted to lead a time. The challenge is in fact more in such cases. It is not that difficult for employees to accept someone who is completely new to them rather than reporting to someone who was their colleague at some point of time and now their reporting authority. Promotions should be linked to individual concerned's track record, past performances, behavioural skills, attitude and so on. Employees would never accept someone as their leader who has never performed but is management's favourite. Trust me, in due course of time , you would face severe problems which would not only lead to good employees quitting and moving ahead but also unsatisfied employees who are there with the organization just to kill time and money.

Management also needs to give space to all the team leaders. Every individual has his/her own style of working. Do not interfere much. You need to give some time to an individual to perform and prove himself/herself. How can you expect a person to perform extraordinarily in just one month? Even the best of employee would not be able to deliver in a very short period. A boss needs one to two months to understand his employees and another one month to make them work and also extract the best out of them.

Give them some freedom and authority. There are organizations where leaders are appointed just to prepare reports, excels and handle the grievances of their team members. For every small approval, they need to discuss with the top management. Trust me, this way managers feel handicapped. Let them take decisions on their own. Management needs to trust and have faith in leaders, vertical heads, team managers and so on. If you do not trust them, then you should not appoint them at the first place. In case of issues, discuss with the leaders first rather than directly interacting with the team members. No one would like and accept it. Give them budgets, deadlines, well defined roles and responsibilities and a good team and let them work in their own way. You would definitely see the difference in a short span of time.

The cliché that leaders are made and not born signifies the fact that leadership and exceptional leadership at that can be within reach of anyone provided they do the steps needed for effective leadership right. To start with, leaders need a vision, which they can then use to inspire their followers and employees. Of course, there are many who believe that visionary leadership is the exclusive domain of particular individuals because of their unique abilities. However, our contention is that vision can be actualized by anyone who works hard, pays attention to detail, and combines both big picture thinking with nuts and bolts execution. We believe that to actualize exceptional leadership, one need not be a product of the leading business schools or engineering colleges. On the contrary, leadership can be actualized through initiation of the vision, sustaining the momentum, and carrying through the implementation. In other words, having vision is not enough and being hardworking is also not enough in isolation. At the same time, having a big picture focus is not enough if the nuts and bolts execution is not rigorous. This means that a successful leader has to have all of these qualities as well as an ability to spot the trends as they emerge or in other words, have the ability to lead from the future as it emerges.

Examples of Successes and Failures from the Corporate World

There are many examples of leaders who had the vision but not the other qualities. Similarly, others were good at execution but lacked vision and trend-spotting abilities. The legendary Lee Iacocca who served in Ford Motors and then Chrysler was a leader who had all the qualities. In more recent times, Steve Jobs was one leader who had all these and crucially the ability to anticipate the future. In Asia, the Infosys founders are examples of leaders who actualized their vision, had the big picture as well as the hands on implementation skills, and were attentive to detail. Similarly, Ratan Tata is one leader who combined all these traits to turnaround a conglomerate that was losing direction and making it competitive again. Of course, there are also failures like Carly Fiona of Hewlett Packard who failed to transform the company and in recent months, Steve Ballmer who failed to leverage on the internet boom to steer Microsoft into a leadership position in the Tablet PC and Smartphone market. In both these cases, the missing element was execution and implementation. In the case of Ballmer, it is surprising that he could not follow through on his and Bill Gates' vision, as he was essentially a nuts and bolts leader who rose to the top. In the case of Carly Fiona, the failure was mostly being unable to see the big picture and implement the change. Of course, to be fair to her, it must be said that the board and key sections of the employees were not completely with her when she attempted the transformation.

Examples of Success and Failure from the Political World

Apart from these leaders, the example of Lee Kuan Yew in the administrative sphere is worth noting. Yew who was one of the founders of Singapore transformed the city-state from a backwater infested with crime and addiction to a booming mega polis that has the highest per capita GDP in the world. In Yew's case, he had the vision, the discipline, the focus, and the attention to detail combined with the big picture thinking that helped him transform Singapore into what it is now. On the other hand, the former Defense Secretary of the United States, Donald Rumsfeld, failed because he could not follow through and implement his vision that is now proven a game changer. These two contrasting leaders offer us lessons on how all the three themes that are the focus of needs to be in balance for exceptional leadership.

Part : I
Motivation

- **What is Motivation ?**

Motivation is the word derived from the word 'motive' which means needs, desires, wants or drives within the individuals. It is the process of stimulating people to actions to accomplish the goals. In the work goal context the psychological factors stimulating the people's behaviour can be -

- desire for money
- success
- recognition
- job-satisfaction
- team work, etc

One of the most important functions of management is to create willingness amongst the employees to perform in the best of their abilities. Therefore the role of a leader is to arouse interest in performance of employees in their jobs. The process of motivation consists of three stages:-

1. A felt need or drive
2. A stimulus in which needs have to be aroused
3. When needs are satisfied, the satisfaction or accomplishment of goals.

Therefore, we can say that motivation is a psychological phenomenon which means needs and wants of the individuals have to be tackled by framing an incentive plan.

- **Maslow's Need Hierarchy Model**

Human Behaviour is goal-directed. Motivation cause goal-directed behaviour. It is through motivation that needs can be handled and tackled purposely. This can be understood by understanding the hierarchy of needs by manager. The needs of individual serves as a driving force in human behaviour. Therefore, a manager must understand the "hierarchy of needs". Maslow has proposed "The Need Hierarchy Model".

```
                                                    ┌──────────────┐
                                                    │ Self-        │
                                                    │ actualization│
                                                    │ Needs        │
                                          ┌────────┐└──────────────┘
                                          │ Esteem │
                                          │ Needs  │
                                ┌────────┐└────────┘
                                │ Social │
                                │ Needs  │
                      ┌─────────┘────────┘
                      │ Security │
                      │ Needs    │
          ┌───────────┘──────────┘
          │ Physiological │
          │ Needs         │
          └───────────────┘
```

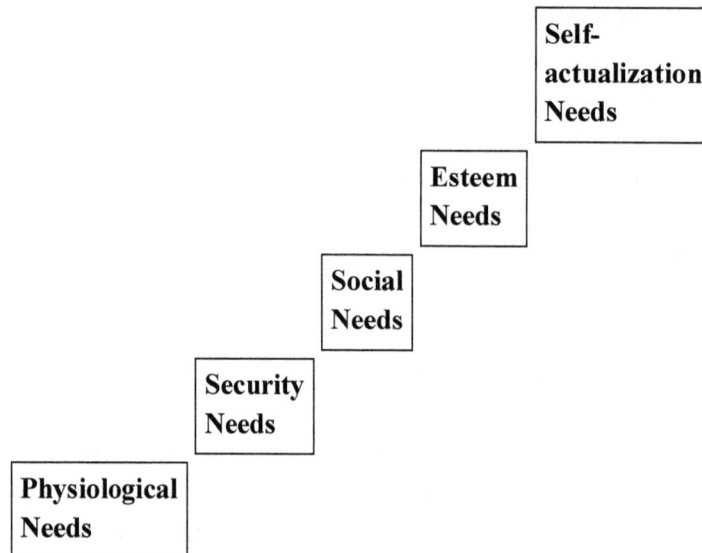

FIGURE - Maslow's Need Hierarchy Model

The needs have been classified into the following in order:

1. **Physiological needs-** These are the basic needs of an individual which includes food, clothing, shelter, air, water, etc. These needs relate to the survival and maintenance of human life.

2. **Safety needs-** These needs are also important for human beings. Everybody wants job security, protection against danger, safety of property, etc.

3. **Social needs-** These needs emerge from society. Man is a social animal. These needs become important. For example- love, affection, belongingness, friendship, conversation, etc.

4. **Esteem needs-** These needs relate to desire for self-respect, recognition and respect from others.

5. **Self-actualization needs-** These are the needs of the highest order and these needs are found in those person whose previous four needs are satisfied. This will include need for social service, meditation.

• **Motivation Incentives - Incentives to motivate employees**
   Incentive is an act or promise for greater action. It is also called

as a stimulus to greater action. Incentives are something which are given in addition to wagers. It means additional remuneration or benefit to an employee in recognition of achievement or better work. Incentives provide a spur or zeal in the employees for better performance. It is a natural thing that nobody acts without a purpose behind. Therefore, a hope for a reward is a powerful incentive to motivate employees. Besides monetary incentive, there are some other stimuli which can drive a person to better. This will include job satisfaction, job security, job promotion, and pride for accomplishment. Therefore, incentives really can sometimes work to accomplish the goals of a concern. The need of incentives can be many:-

1.   To increase productivity,
2.   To drive or arouse a stimulus work,
3.   To enhance commitment in work performance,
4.   To psychologically satisfy a person which leads to job satisfaction,
5.   To shape the behavior or outlook of subordinate towards work,
6.   To inculcate zeal and enthusiasm towards work,
7.   To get the maximum of their capabilities so that they are exploited and utilized maximally.

Therefore, management has to offer the following two categories of incentives to motivate employees:

1.   Monetary incentives- Those incentives which satisfy the subordinates by providing them rewards in terms of rupees. Money has been recognized as a chief source of satisfying the needs of people. Money is also helpful to satisfy the social needs by possessing various material items. Therefore, money not only satisfies psychological needs but also the security and social needs. Therefore, in many factories, various wage plans and bonus schemes are introduced to motivate and stimulate the people to work.

2.   Non-monetary incentives- Besides the monetary incentives, there are certain non-financial incentives which can satisfy the ego and self- actualization needs of employees. The incentives which cannot be measured in terms of money are under the category of "Non-monetary incentives". Whenever a manager has to satisfy the

77

psychological needs of the subordinates, he makes use of non-financial incentives. Non- financial incentives can be of the following types:-

    a.   **Security of service-** Job security is an incentive which provides great motivation to employees. If his job is secured, he will put maximum efforts to achieve the objectives of the enterprise. This also helps since he is very far off from mental tension and he can give his best to the enterprise.

    b.   **Praise or recognition-** The praise or recognition is another non- financial incentive which satisfies the ego needs of the employees. Sometimes praise becomes more effective than any other incentive. The employees will respond more to praise and try to give the best of their abilities to a concern.

    c.   **Suggestion scheme-** The organization should look forward to taking suggestions and inviting suggestion schemes from the subordinates. This inculcates a spirit of participation in the employees. This can be done by publishing various points written by employees to improve the work environment which can be published in various magazines of the company. This also is helpful to motivate the employees to feel important and they can also be in search for innovative methods which can be applied for better work methods. This ultimately helps in growing a concern and adapting new methods of operations.

    d.   **Job enrichment-** Job enrichment is another non-monetary incentive in which the job of a worker can be enriched. This can be done by increasing his responsibilities, giving him an important designation, increasing the content and nature of the work. This way efficient worker can get challenging jobs in which they can prove their worth. This also helps in the greatest motivation of the efficient employees.

    e.   **Promotion opportunities-** Promotion is an effective tool to increase the spirit to work in a concern. If the employees are provided opportunities for the advancement and growth, they feel satisfied and contented and they become more committed to the organization.

    The above non-financial tools can be framed effectively by giving due concentration to the role of employees. A combination of financial and non- financial incentives help together in bringing motivation and zeal to work in a concern.

Positive Incentives

Positive incentives are those incentives which provide a positive assurance for fulfilling the needs and wants. Positive incentives generally have an optimistic attitude behind and they are generally given to satisfy the psychological requirements of employees. For example-promotion, praise, recognition, perks and allowances, etc. It is positive by nature.

Negative Incentives

Negative incentives are those whose purpose is to correct the mistakes or defaults of employees. The purpose is to rectify mistakes in order to get effective results. Negative incentive is generally resorted to when positive incentive does not works and a psychological set back has to be given to employees. It is negative by nature. For example-demotion, transfer, fines, penalties.

- **Importance of Motivation**

    Motivation is a very important for an organization because of the following benefits it provides:-

    1. **Puts human resources into action**

        Every concern requires physical, financial and human resources to accomplish the goals. It is through motivation that the human resources can be utilized by making full use of it. This can be done by building willingness in employees to work. This will help the enterprise in securing best possible utilization of resources.

    2. **Improves level of efficiency of employees**

        The level of a subordinate or a employee does not only depend upon his qualifications and abilities. For getting best of his work performance, the gap between ability and willingness has to be filled which helps in improving the level of performance of subordinates. This will result into-

        a. Increase in productivity,

        b. Reducing cost of operations, and

        c. Improving overall efficiency.

    3. **Leads to achievement of organizational goals**

The goals of an enterprise can be achieved only when the following factors take place :-

a.   There is best possible utilization of resources,

b.   There is a co-operative work environment,

c.   The employees are goal-directed and they act in a purposive manner,

d.   Goals can be achieved if co-ordination and co-operation takes place simultaneously which can be effectively done through motivation.

4.   Builds friendly relationship

Motivation is an important factor which brings employees satisfaction. This can be done by keeping into mind and framing an incentive plan for the benefit of the employees. This could initiate the following things:

a.   Monetary and non-monetary incentives,

b.   Promotion opportunities for employees,

c.   Disincentives for inefficient employees.

In order to build a cordial, friendly atmosphere in a concern, the above steps should be taken by a manager. This would help in:

I.   Effective co-operation which brings stability,

II.   Industrial dispute and unrest in employees will reduce,

III.   The employees will be adaptable to the changes and there will be no resistance to the change,

IV.   This will help in providing a smooth and sound concern in which individual interests will coincide with the organizational interests,

V.   This will result in profit maximization through increased productivity.

- **Leads to stability of work force**

Stability of workforce is very important from the point of view of reputation and goodwill of a concern. The employees can remain loyal to the enterprise only when they have a feeling of participation in the management. The skills and efficiency of employees will always be of advantage to employees as well as employees. This will lead to a good public image in the market which will attract competent and qualified people into a concern. As it is said, "Old is gold" which suffices with the role of motivation here, the older the people, more the experience and their adjustment into a concern which can be of benefit to the enterprise.

From the above discussion, we can say that motivation is an internal feeling which can be understood only by manager since he is in close contact with the employees. Needs, wants and desires are inter-related and they are the driving force to act. These needs can be understood by the manager and he can frame motivation plans accordingly. We can say that motivation therefore is a continuous process since motivation process is based on needs which are unlimited. The process has to be continued throughout.

We can summarize by saying that motivation is important both to an individual and a business. **Motivation is important to an individual as:**

1. Motivation will help him achieve his personal goals.
2. If an individual is motivated, he will have job satisfaction.
3. Motivation will help in self-development of individual.
4. An individual would always gain by working with a dynamic team.

Similarly, **motivation is important to a business as:**

1. The more motivated the employees are, the more empowered the team is.
2. The more is the team work and individual employee contribution, more profitable and successful is the business.
3. During period of amendments, there will be more adaptability and creativity.
4. Motivation will lead to an optimistic and challenging attitude at work place.

Motivation and Morale - Relationship and Differences

Motivation can be defined as the total satisfaction derived by an individual from his job, his work-group, his superior, the organization he works for and the environment. It generally relates to the feeling of individual's comfort, happiness and satisfaction.

According to Davis, "Morale is a mental condition of groups and individuals which determines their attitude."

In short, morale is a fusion of employees' attitudes, behaviours, manifestation of views and opinions - all taken together in their work scenarios, exhibiting the employees' feelings towards work, working terms and relation with their employers. Morale includes employees' attitudes on and specific reaction to their job.

There are two states of morale:

High morale - High morale implies determination at work- an essential in achievement of management objectives. High morale results in:

- ✓ A keen teamwork on part of the employees.
- ✓ Organizational Commitment and a sense of belongingness in the employees mind.
- ✓ Immediate conflict identification and resolution.
- ✓ Healthy and safe work environment.
- ✓ Effective communication in the organization.
- ✓ Increase in productivity.
- ✓ Greater motivation.

Low morale - Low morale has following features:

- ✓ Greater grievances and conflicts in organization.
- ✓ High rate of employee absenteeism and turnover.
- ✓ Dissatisfaction with the superiors and employers.
- ✓ Poor working conditions.
- ✓ Employees frustration.
- ✓ Decrease in productivity.
- ✓ Lack of motivation.

Though motivation and morale are closely related concepts, they are different in following ways:

While motivation is an internal-psychological drive of an individual which urges him to behave in a specific manner, morale is more of a group scenario.

Higher motivation often leads to higher morale of employees, but high morale does not essentially result in greatly motivated employees as to have a positive attitude towards all factors of work situation may not essentially force the employees to work more efficiently.

While motivation is an individual concept, morale is a group concept. Thus, motivation takes into consideration the individual differences among the employees, and morale of the employees can be increased by taking those factors into consideration which influence group scenario or total work settings.

Motivation acquires primary concern in every organization, while morale is a secondary phenomenon because high motivation essentially leads to higher productivity while high morale may not necessarily lead to higher productivity.

Things tied to morale are usually things that are just part of the work environment, and things tied to motivation are tied to the performance of the individual.

- **Staff Motivation - Motivation Tips for Employees**

Employees are the building blocks of an organization. Organizational success depends on the collective efforts of the employees. The employees will collectively contribute to organizational growth when they are motivated.

Below mentioned are some tips for motivating the staff/employees in an organization:

Evaluate yourself- In order to motivate, encourage and control your staff's behaviour, it is essential to understand, encourage and control your own behaviour as a manager. Work upon utilizing your strengths and opportunities to neutralize and lower the negative impact of your weaknesses and organizational threats. The manager should adopt the approach "You're OK - I'm OK".

Be familiar with your staff- The manager should be well acquainted with his staff. The more and the better he knows his staff, the simpler it is to get them involved in the job as well as in achieving the team and organizational goals. This will also invite staff's commitment and loyalty. A cordial superior-subordinate relationship is a key factor in job-satisfaction.

Provide the employees certain benefits- Give your staff some financial and other benefits. Give them bonuses, pay them for overtime, and give them health and family insurance benefits. Make sure they get breaks from work. Let them enjoy vacations and holidays.

Participate in new employees induction programme- Induction proceeds with recruitment advertising. At this point of time, the potential entrants start creating their own impressions and desires about the job and the organization. The manner in which the selection is conducted and the consequent recruitment process will either build or damage the impression about the job and organization. Thus, the manager must have a say in framing the advertisement and also in the selection and recruitment process. After the decision about the candidate is made, the manager must take personal interest in the selected joinee's joining date, the family relocation issues, cost of removal, etc. Being observed by the new recruit and your entire team / staff to be involved completely, will ensure a persuasive entry in the organization.

Provide feedback to the staff constantly- The staff members are keen to know how they are performing. Try giving a regular and constructive feedback to your staff. This will be more acceptable by the staff. Do not base the feedback on assumptions, but on facts and personal observations. Do not indulge in favouritism or comparing the employee with some one else. Sit with your staff on daily or weekly basis and make sure that feedback happens. This will help in boosting employee's morale and will thus motivate the staff.

Acknowledge your staff on their achievements- A pat on the back, some words of praise, and giving a note of credit to the employee / staff member at personal level with some form of broad publicity can motivate the staff a lot. Make it a point to mention the staff's outstanding achievements in official newsletters or organization's journal. Not only acknowledge the employee with highest contribution, but also acknowledge the employee who meets and over exceeds the targets.

Ensure effective time management- Having control over time ensures that things are done in right manner. Motivate your staff to have "closed" times, i.e., few hours when there are no interruptions for the staff in performing their job role so that they can concentrate on the job, and "open" times when the staff freely communicate and interact. Plan one to one sessions of interaction with your staff where they can ask their queries and also can get your attention and, thereby, they will not feel neglected. This all will work in long run to motivate the staff.

Have stress management techniques in your organization- Create an environment in which you and your staff can work within optimum pressure levels. Ensure an optimistic attitude towards stress in the workplace. Have training sessions on stress management, and ensure a follow-up with group meetings on the manner stress can be lowered at work. Give your staff autonomy in work. Identify the stress symptoms in employees and try to deal with them.

Use counselling technique- The employees' / staff feelings towards the work, their peer, their superiors and towards the future can be effectively dealt through the staff counseling. Counselling provides an environment, incentive and support which enable the employee to achieve his identity.

Give the employees learning opportunities- Employees should consistently learn new skills on the job. It has been well said by someone that with people hopping jobs more often than required and organizations no longer giving job security to employees, the young blood employees specifically realize that continuing learning is the best way to remain employable. Opportunities should be given to the employees to develop their skills and competencies and to make best use of their skills. Link the staff goals with the organizational goals.

Set an example for your staff / subordinates- Be a role model for your staff. The staff would learn from what you do and not from what you say / claim. The way you interact with your clients / customers and how do you react later after the interaction is over have an impact upon the staff. The staff more closely observes your non-verbal communication (gestures, body language). Being unpunctual, wasting the organization's capital, mismanaging organization's physical equipments, asking the staff to do your personal work, etc. all have a negative impact on the staff. Try setting an example for your staff to follow.

Smile often- Smiling can have a tremendous effect on boosting the morale of the staff. A smiling superior creates an optimistic and motivating work environment. Smiling is an essential component of the body language of confidence, acceptance and boldness. Smile consistently, naturally and often, to demonstrate that you feel good and positive about the staff who works for you. It encourages new ideas and feedback from the staff. The staff does not feel hesitant and threatened to discuss their views this way.

Listen effectively- Listening attentively is a form of recognizing and appreciating the person who is talking. Reciprocal / Mutual listening develops cordial and healthy personal relationships on which the employee / staff development rests. If the managers do not listen attentively to the subordinates, the morale of the subordinates lowers down and they do not feel like sharing their ideas or giving their views. Effective listening by the manager boosts up the employees' morale and thus motivates them.

Ensure effective communication- In order to motivate your staff, indulge in effective communication such as avoid using anger expressions, utilize questioning techniques to know staff's mindset and analysis rather than ordering the staff what to do, base your judgements on facts and not on assumptions, use relaxed and steady tone of voice, listen effectively and be positive and helpful in your responses. Share your views with the staff.

Develop and encourage creativity- The staff should be encouraged to develop the creativity skills so as to solve organizational problems. Give them time and resources for developing creativity. Let them hold constant brainstorming sessions. Invite ideas and suggestions from the staff. They may turn out to be very productive.

Don't be rigid. Be flexible- Introduce flexibility in work. Allow for flexible working hours if possible. Let the employees work at home occasionally if need arises. Do not be rigid in accepting ideas from your staff. Stimulate flexible attitudes in the employees who are accountable to you by asking what changes they would like to bring about if given a chance.

Adopt job enrichment- Job enrichment implies giving room for a better quality of working life. It means facilitating people to achieve self-development, fame and success through a more challenging and interesting job which provides more promotional and advancement opportunities. Give employees more freedom in job, involve them in decision-making process, show them loyalty and celebrate their achievements.

Respect your team- Respect not only the employees' rights to share and express their views, and to be themselves, but their time too. This will ensure that the employees respect you and your time. Make the staff feel that they are respected not just as employees / workers but as individuals too.

- **Workplace Motivation - Carrot or Stick approach doesn't work anymore**

"I am in this job because I have no other option." If this is what an employee of your company feels, read on to know how this statement can be changed to something more positive - "I love what I do."

First things first - whose responsibility is it to ensure that an employee loves his job? While an employee would say - the employer, the human resource experts have a different point of view which sounds fair. It's both the employer and the employee who should work together to make work fun for each other.

It is interesting to know here, that employees do not rank 'salary' as the top factor in determining whether they like their jobs or not. What is important to them then - the opportunity to do what is 'important'. Almost all the employees would like to feel part of the big picture and would want to contribute to the organizational goals in some way or the other. Doing the mundane, routine work will never excite them - what excites them is - work that challenges them to use their talent. Right Management Consultants conducted a survey sometime back and found that 83% of about 500 workers surveyed were motivated by "challenges at work".

Also, as per an executive editor of the Harvard Business Review, while salary and promotions could do a great job of demotivating people if handled ineffectively, they aren't so much effective in motivating people.

So then what needs to be done for effective motivation at workplace?

Link Rewards directly to Performance- An organization should adopt a fair reward structure which provides incentive to the most deserving employee. Have an incentive structure in place doesn't solve the problem... what makes it workable is the employees trust in the system and believe that they will be rewarded if they perform well.

Compliment employees- Even though an employee's name has not appeared in the list of people getting incentives, go ahead and compliment that employee for a job well done - no matter how small. There is nothing more satisfying to an employee than a pat on his back.

Be transparent- While there may be some strategic decisions which you might want to share with the employees at a later stage, make sure employees do not give in to the rumours. Stay in touch with the employees.

Work on your PDP- Every employee is responsible for his / her own career. He / she should work towards his 'Personal Development Plan' [PDP] as discussed and agreed by his manager. Find out what are the training company offers and which is best suited to his development needs. How this will motivate you - remember training always increase your marketability and enhance your career.

Participate and Network- Employees - Remember you work for a company where a one-on-one attention might not be possible. Do not wait for an invitation to participate in a discussion. If you are a part of a forum, then you have full right to express your opinion and be a part of the process. Expressing yourself is a good way of motivating yourself.

Self Motivation at Work

Self-motivation is a power that drives us to keep moving ahead. It encourages continuous learning and success, whatever be the scenario. Self-motivation is a primary means of realizing our goals and progressing. It is basically related to our inventiveness in setting dynamic goals for ourselves, and our faith that we possess the required skills and competencies for achieving those challenging goals. We often feel the need for self-motivation.

Following are the ways/techniques for self-motivation:

Communicate and talk to get motivated: Communicating with someone can boost up your energy and make you go on track. Talk with optimistic and motivated individuals. They can be your colleagues, friends, wife, or any one with whom you can share your ideas.

Remain optimistic: When facing hurdles; we always make efforts to find how to overcome them. Also, one should understand the good in bad.

Discover your interest area: If you lack interest in current task, you should not proceed and continue with it. If an individual has no interest in the task, but if it is essential to perform, he should correlate it with a bigger ultimate goal.

Self-acknowledgement: One should know when his motivation level is saturated and he feels like on top of the world. There will be a blueprint that once an individual acknowledge, he can proceed with his job and can grow.

Monitor and record your success: Maintain a success bar for the assignments you are currently working on. When you observe any progress, you will obviously want to foster it.

Uplift energy level: Energy is very essential for self-motivation. Do regular exercises. Have proper sleep. Have tea/coffee during breaks to refresh you.

Assist, support and motivate others: Discuss and share your views and ideas with your friends and peers and assist them in getting motivated. When we observe others performing good, it will keep us motivated too. Invite feedback from others on your achievements.

Encourage learning: Always encourage learning. Read and grasp the logic and jist of the reading. Learning makes an individual more confident in commencing new assignments.

Break your bigger goals into smaller goals: Set a short time deadline for each smaller goal so as to achieve bigger goal on time.

- **Team Motivation - Tips for Motivating Team**

A group heading towards a common objective will perform best when it is motivated as a team. Team motivation is determined by how well the team members' needs and requirements are met by the team.

Some tips for effective team motivation are as follows:

The team's objective should well align and synchronize with the team members needs and requirements.

Give in written the team's mission and ensure that all understand it (as mission is a foundation based on which the team performs).

For maintaining motivation, the team should be given challenges (which must be difficult but achievable) consistently.

Giving a team responsibility accompanied by authority can also be a good motivator for the team to perform.

The team should be provided with growth opportunities. The team's motivation level is high when the team members feel that they are being promoted, their skills and competencies are being enhanced, and they are learning new things consistently.

Effective and true leaders can develop environment for the team to motivate itself. They provide spur for self- actualization behaviours of team members.

Devote quality/productive time to your team. Have an optimistic and good relation with your team members. This will make you more acquainted with them and you can get knowledge of how well they are performing their job. Welcome their views and ideas as they may be fruitful and it will also boost their morale.

Motivation is all about empowerment. The skills and competencies of the team members should be fully utilized. Empowering the team members makes them accountable for their own actions.

Provide feedback to the team consistently. Become their mentor. Give the team recognition for good and outstanding performance. Give the team a constructive and not negative feedback.

Discover and offset the factors which discourage team spirit such as too many conflicts, lethargy, team members' escape from responsibilities, lack of job satisfaction, etc.

- **The Role of Motivation in Organizational Behavior**
  Some Factors that can Motivate Employees

The organizational structure is another aspect that can motivate employees. For instance, it has been found that flat organizations as opposed to hierarchical organizations motivate employees more. Next, the organizational culture plays an important role in motivating employees. The examples of Google, Facebook, and startup companies where the organizational culture is open and collegiate are relevant in this regard. Third, the HR managers have an important role to play in motivating employees by interacting with them, finding their grievances, and proposing solutions to behavioral problems. There are many multinationals like Fidelity where the HR managers hold one on one sessions with the employees to foster an open and inclusive culture where employees do not hold anything back and where they are encouraged to be as forthright as possible. Fourth, organizations that promote diversity as an organizational imperative are known to motivate women employees who feel less threatened and less insecure than in organizations where bias and prejudice are rampant. Fifth, many organizations have the habit of saying one thing and doing something else altogether which means that they are hypocritical in their approach. Such organizations cannot motivate the employees particularly at the lower levels since the fresh recruits and those with less experience often look to the senior managers and the leadership for integrity and consistency.

Salary and Benefits are not the only Motivators

Having covered the various aspects of how the organizations can motivate the employees, it needs to be mentioned that mere reliance on salary and benefits cannot motivate employees completely. With the advent of the software and services sector, the attraction of being sent onsite has become an important motivator for the employees who when given the chance to go onsite ramp up on their performance noticeably. Apart from this, the fact that the brand image of the organization makes a lot of difference to the motivation levels of the employees is another factor. For instance, many graduates have their own preferences for dream companies or companies that they would like to work in after graduation. This important motivator attracts the best talent to those companies that are often viewed as the benchmark for industry peers. Of course, if the image does not meet up to reality or if the hype is without substance, many employees lose motivation to work in such companies.

Concluding Thoughts

Finally, as discussed above, there is no set formula on what organizations can do or cannot do to motivate the employees. The best approach would be to let employees find their own niche within the organization and let them actualize their potential instead of forcing them to do work that is not to their liking. Apart from this, many industry veterans are also of the view that employees have to find their company that suits them and hence, clinging on to jobs that do not motivate them is counterproductive.

- ### Motivational Challenges

Motivation seems to be a simple function of management in books, but in practice it is more challenging. **The reasons for motivation being challenging job are as follows:**

- One of the main reasons of motivation being a challenging job is due to the changing workforce. The employees become a part of their organization with various needs and expectations. Different employees have different beliefs, attitudes, values, backgrounds and thinking. But all the organizations are not aware of the diversity in their workforce and thus are not aware and clear about different ways of motivating their diverse workforce.

- Employees motives cannot be seen, they can only be presumed. Suppose, there are two employees in a team showing varying performance despite being of same age group, having same educational qualifications and same work experience. The reason being what motivates one employee may not seem motivating to other.

- Motivation of employees becomes challenging especially when the organizations have considerably changed the job role of the employees, or have lessened the hierarchy levels of hierarchy, or have chucked out a significant number of employees in the name of down-sizing or right-sizing. Certain firms have chosen to hire and fire and paying for performance strategies nearly giving up motivational efforts. These strategies are unsuccessful in making an individual overreach himself.

- The vigorous nature of needs also pose challenge to a manager in motivating his subordinates. This is because an employee at a certain point of time has diverse needs and expectations. Also, these needs and expectations keep on changing and might also clash with each other. For instance-the employees who spend extra time at work for meeting their needs for accomplishment might discover that the extra time spent by them clash with their social neds and with the need for affiliation.

- **Essentials / Features of a Good Motivation System**

Motivation is a state of mind. High motivation leads to high morale and greater production. A motivated employee gives his best to the organization. He stays loyal and committed to the organization. A sound motivation system in an organization should have the following features:

Superior performance should be reasonably rewarded and should be duely acknowledged. If the performance is not consistently up to the mark, then the system must make provisions for penalties.

The employees must be dealt in a fair and just manner. The grievances and obstacles faced by them must be dealt instantly and fairly.

Carrot and stick approach should be implemented to motivate both efficient and inefficient employees. The employees should treat negative consequences (such as fear of punishment) as stick, an outside push and move away from it. They should take positive consequences (such as reward) as carrot, an inner pull and move towards it.

Performance appraisal system should be very effective.

Ensure flexibility in working arrangements.

A sound motivation system must be correlated to organizational goals. Thus, the individual/employee goals must be harmonized with the organizational goals.

The motivational system must be modified to the situation and to the organization.

A sound motivation system requires modifying the nature of individual's jobs. The jobs should be redesigned or restructured according to the requirement of situation. Any of the alternatives to job specialization - job rotation, job enlargement, job enrichment, etc. could be used.

The management approach should be participative. All the subordinates and employees should be involved in decision- making process.

The motivation system should involve monetary as well as non-monetary rewards. The monetary rewards should be correlated to performance. Performance should be based on the employees' action towards the goals, and not on the fame of employees.

"Motivate yourself to motivate your employees" should be the managerial approach.

The managers must understand and identify the motivators for each employee.

Sound motivation system should encourage supportive supervision whereby the supervisors share their views and experiences with their subordinates, listen to the subordinates views, and assist the subordinates in performing the designated job.

- **Classical Theories of Motivation**

The motivation concepts were mainly developed around 1950's. Three main theories were made during this period. These three classical theories are-

> Maslow's hierarchy of needs theory
>
> Herzberg's Two factor theory
>
> Theory X and Theory Y

These theories are building blocks of the contemporary theories developed later. The working mangers and learned professionals till date use these classical theories to explain the concept of employee motivation.

Maslow's Hierarchy of Needs Theory

Abraham Maslow is well renowned for proposing the Hierarchy of Needs Theory in 1943. This theory is a classical depiction of human motivation. This theory is based on the assumption that there is a hierarchy of five needs within each individual. The urgency of these needs varies. These five needs are as follows-

Physiological needs- These are the basic needs of air, water, food, clothing and shelter. In other words, physiological needs are the needs for basic amenities of life.

Safety needs- Safety needs include physical, environmental and emotional safety and protection. For instance- Job security, financial security, protection from animals, family security, health security, etc.

Social needs- Social needs include the need for love, affection, care, belongingness, and friendship.

Esteem needs- Esteem needs are of two types: internal esteem needs (self- respect, confidence, competence, achievement and freedom) and external esteem needs (recognition, power, status, attention and admiration).

Self-actualization need- This include the urge to become what you are capable of becoming / what you have the potential to become. It includes the need for growth and self-contentment. It also includes desire for gaining more knowledge, social- service, creativity and being aesthetic. The self- actualization needs are never fully satiable. As an individual grows psychologically, opportunities keep cropping up to continue growing.

According to Maslow, individuals are motivated by unsatisfied needs. As each of these needs is significantly satisfied, it drives and forces the next need to emerge. Maslow grouped the five needs into two categories - Higher-order needs and Lower-order needs. The physiological and the safety needs constituted the lower-order needs. These lower-order needs are mainly satisfied externally. The social, esteem, and self-actualization needs constituted the higher-order needs. These higher-order needs are generally satisfied internally, i.e., within an individual. Thus, we can conclude that during boom period, the employees lower-order needs are significantly met.

Implications of Maslow's Hierarchy of Needs Theory for Managers

As far as the physiological needs are concerned, the managers should give employees appropriate salaries to purchase the basic necessities of life. Breaks and eating opportunities should be given to employees.

As far as the safety needs are concerned, the managers should provide the employees job security, safe and hygienic work environment, and retirement benefits so as to retain them.

As far as social needs are concerned, the management should encourage teamwork and organize social events.

As far as esteem needs are concerned, the managers can appreciate and reward employees on accomplishing and exceeding their targets. The management can give the deserved employee higher job rank / position in the organization.

As far as self-actualization needs are concerned, the managers can give the employees challenging jobs in which the employees' skills and competencies are fully utilized. Moreover, growth opportunities can be given to them so that they can reach the peak.

The managers must identify the need level at which the employee is existing and then those needs can be utilized as push for motivation.

Limitations of Maslow's Theory

It is essential to note that not all employees are governed by same set of needs. Different individuals may be driven by different needs at same point of time. It is always the most powerful unsatisfied need that motivates an individual.

The theory is not empirically supported.

The theory is not applicable in case of starving artist as even if the artist's basic needs are not satisfied, he will still strive for recognition and achievement.

- **Herzberg's Two-Factor Theory of Motivation**

In 1959, Frederick Herzberg, a behavioural scientist proposed a two-factor theory or the motivator-hygiene theory. According to Herzberg, there are some job factors that result in satisfaction while there are other job factors that prevent dissatisfaction. According to Herzberg, the opposite of "Satisfaction" is "No satisfaction" and the opposite of "Dissatisfaction" is "No Dissatisfaction".

Herzbergs view of satisfaction and dissatisfaction

Herzberg classified these job factors into two categories-

Hygiene factors- Hygiene factors are those job factors which are essential for existence of motivation at workplace. These do not lead to positive satisfaction for long-term. But if these factors are absent / if these factors are non-existant at workplace, then they lead to

96

dissatisfaction. In other words, hygiene factors are those factors which when adequate/reasonable in a job, pacify the employees and do not make them dissatisfied. These factors are extrinsic to work. Hygiene factors are also called as dissatisfiers or maintenance factors as they are required to avoid dissatisfaction. These factors describe the job environment/scenario. The hygiene factors symbolized the physiological needs which the individuals wanted and expected to be fulfilled. Hygiene factors include:

Pay - The pay or salary structure should be appropriate and reasonable. It must be equal and competitive to those in the same industry in the same domain.

Company Policies and administrative policies - The company policies should not be too rigid. They should be fair and clear. It should include flexible working hours, dress code, breaks, vacation, etc.

Fringe benefits - The employees should be offered health care plans (mediclaim), benefits for the family members, employee help programmes, etc.

Physical Working conditions - The working conditions should be safe, clean and hygienic. The work equipments should be updated and well-maintained.

Status - The employees' status within the organization should be familiar and retained.

Interpersonal relations - The relationship of the employees with his peers, superiors and subordinates should be appropriate and acceptable. There should be no conflict or humiliation element present.

Job Security - The organization must provide job security to the employees.

Motivational factors- According to Herzberg, the hygiene factors cannot be regarded as motivators. The motivational factors yield positive satisfaction. These factors are inherent to work. These factors motivate the employees for a superior performance. These factors are called satisfiers. These are factors involved in performing the job. Employees find these factors intrinsically rewarding. The motivators symbolized the psychological needs that were perceived as an additional benefit. Motivational factors include:

Recognition - The employees should be praised and recognized for their accomplishments by the managers.

Sense of achievement - The employees must have a sense of achievement. This depends on the job. There must be a fruit of some sort in the job.

Growth and promotional opportunities - There must be growth and advancement opportunities in an organization to motivate the employees to perform well.

Responsibility - The employees must hold themselves responsible for the work. The managers should give them ownership of the work. They should minimize control but retain accountability.

Meaningfulness of the work - The work itself should be meaningful, interesting and challenging for the employee to perform and to get motivated.

Limitations of Two-Factor Theory

The two factor theory is not free from limitations:

The two-factor theory overlooks situational variables.

Herzberg assumed a correlation between satisfaction and productivity. But the research conducted by Herzberg stressed upon satisfaction and ignored productivity.

The theory's reliability is uncertain. Analysis has to be made by the raters. The raters may spoil the findings by analyzing same response in different manner.

No comprehensive measure of satisfaction was used. An employee may find his job acceptable despite the fact that he may hate/object part of his job.

The two factor theory is not free from bias as it is based on the natural reaction of employees when they are enquired the sources of satisfaction and dissatisfaction at work. They will blame dissatisfaction on the external factors such as salary structure, company policies and peer relationship. Also, the employees will give credit to themselves for the satisfaction factor at work.

The theory ignores blue-collar workers. Despite these limitations, Herzberg's Two-Factor theory is acceptable broadly.

Implications of Two-Factor Theory

The Two-Factor theory implies that the managers must stress upon guaranteeing the adequacy of the hygiene factors to avoid employee dissatisfaction. Also, the managers must make sure that the work is stimulating and rewarding so that the employees are motivated to work and perform harder and better. This theory emphasize upon job-enrichment so as to motivate the employees. The job must utilize the employee's skills and competencies to the maximum. Focusing on the motivational factors can improve work-quality.

- **Theory X and Theory Y**

In 1960, Douglas McGregor formulated Theory X and Theory Y suggesting two aspects of human behaviour at work, or in other words, two different views of individuals (employees): one of which is negative, called as Theory X and the other is positive, so called as Theory Y. According to McGregor, the perception of managers on the nature of individuals is based on various assumptions.

Assumptions of Theory X

An average employee intrinsically does not like work and tries to escape it whenever possible.

Since the employee does not want to work, he must be persuaded, compelled, or warned with punishment so as to achieve organizational goals. A close supervision is required on part of managers. The managers adopt a more dictatorial style.

Many employees rank job security on top, and they have little or no aspiration/ ambition.

Employees generally dislike responsibilities.

Employees resist change.

An average employee needs formal direction.

Assumptions of Theory Y

Employees can perceive their job as relaxing and normal. They exercise their physical and mental efforts in an inherent manner in their jobs.

Employees may not require only threat, external control and coercion to work, but they can use self-direction and self-control if they are dedicated and sincere to achieve the organizational objectives.

If the job is rewarding and satisfying, then it will result in employees' loyalty and commitment to organization.

An average employee can learn to admit and recognize the responsibility. In fact, he can even learn to obtain responsibility.

The employees have skills and capabilities. Their logical capabilities should be fully utilized. In other words, the creativity, resourcefulness and innovative potentiality of the employees can be utilized to solve organizational problems.

Thus, we can say that Theory X presents a pessimistic view of employees' nature and behaviour at work, while Theory Y presents an optimistic view of the employees' nature and behaviour at work. If correlate it with Maslow's theory, we can say that Theory X is based on the assumption that the employees emphasize on the physiological needs and the safety needs; while Theory X is based on the assumption that the social needs, esteem needs and the self-actualization needs dominate the employees.

McGregor views Theory Y to be more valid and reasonable than Theory X. Thus, he encouraged cordial team relations, responsible and stimulating jobs, and participation of all in decision-making process.

Implications of Theory X and Theory Y

Quite a few organizations use Theory X today. Theory X encourages use of tight control and supervision. It implies that employees are reluctant to organizational changes. Thus, it does not encourage innovation.

Many organizations are using Theory Y techniques. Theory Y implies that the managers should create and encourage a work environment which provides opportunities to employees to take initiative and self-direction. Employees should be given opportunities to contribute to organizational well-being. Theory Y encourages decentralization of authority, teamwork and participative decision making in an organization. Theory Y searches and discovers the ways in which an employee can make significant contributions in an organization. It harmonizes and matches employees' needs and aspirations with organizational needs and aspirations.

- **Modern Theories of Motivation**

We all are familiar with the classical theories of motivation, but they all are not empirically supported. As far as contemporary theories of motivation are concerned, all are well supported with evidences. Some of the contemporary / modern theories of motivation are explained below:

ERG Theory

- ✓ McClelland's Theory of Needs
- ✓ Goal Setting Theory
- ✓ Reinforcement Theory
- ✓ Equity Theory of Motivation
- ✓ Expectancy Theory of Motivation

ERG Theory of Motivation

To bring Maslow's need hierarchy theory of motivation in synchronization with empirical research, Clayton Alderfer redefined it in his own terms. His rework is called as ERG theory of motivation. He recategorized Maslow's hierarchy of needs into three simpler and broader classes of needs:

- **Existence needs-** These include need for basic material necessities. In short, it includes an individual's physiological and physical safety needs.

- **Relatedness needs-** These include the aspiration individual's have for maintaining significant interpersonal relationships (be it with family, peers or superiors), getting public fame and recognition. Maslow's social needs and external component of esteem needs fall under this class of need.

- **Growth needs-** These include need for self-development and personal growth and advancement. Maslow's self-actualization needs and intrinsic component of esteem needs fall under this category of need.

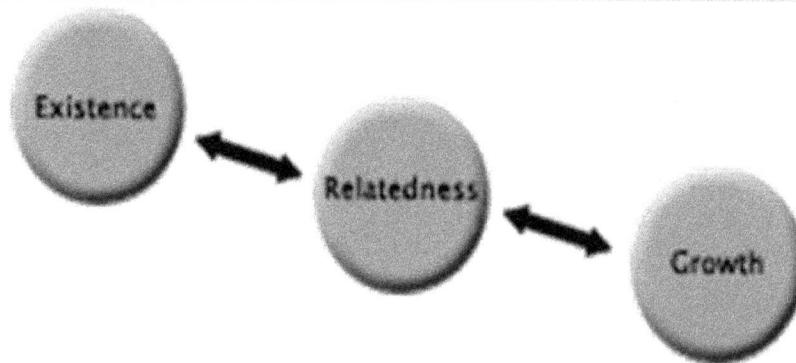

The significance of the three classes of needs may vary for each individual.

- **Difference between Maslow Need Hierarchy Theory and Alderfer's ERG Theory**

ERG Theory states that at a given point of time, more than one need may be operational.

ERG Theory also shows that if the fulfillment of a higher-level need is subdued, there is an increase in desire for satisfying a lower-level need.

According to Maslow, an individual remains at a particular need level until that need is satisfied. While according to ERG theory, if a higher- level need aggravates, an individual may revert to increase the satisfaction of a lower- level need. This is called frustration- regression aspect of ERG theory. For instance- when growth need aggravates, then an individual might be motivated to accomplish the relatedness need and if there are issues in accomplishing relatedness needs, then he might be motivated by the existence needs. Thus, frustration/aggravation can result in regression to a lower-level need.

While Maslow's need hierarchy theory is rigid as it assumes that the needs follow a specific and orderly hierarchy and unless a lower-level need is satisfied, an individual cannot proceed to the higher-level need; ERG Theory of motivation is very flexible as he perceived the needs as a range/variety rather than perceiving them as a hierarchy.

According to Alderfer, an individual can work on growth needs even if his existence or relatedness needs remain unsatisfied. Thus, he gives explanation to the issue of "starving artist" who can struggle for growth even if he is hungry.

Implications of the ERG Theory

Managers must understand that an employee has various needs that must be satisfied at the same time. According to the ERG theory, if the manager concentrates solely on one need at a time, this will not effectively motivate the employee. Also, the frustration- regression aspect of ERG Theory has an added effect on workplace motivation. For instance- if an employee is not provided with growth and advancement opportunities in an organization, he might revert to the relatedness need such as socializing needs and to meet those socializing needs, if the environment or circumstances do not permit, he might revert to the need for money to fulfill those socializing needs. The sooner the manager realizes and discovers this, the more immediate steps they will take to fulfill those needs which are frustrated until such time that the employee can again pursue growth.

Expectancy Theory of Motivation

The expectancy theory was proposed by Victor Vroom of Yale School of Management in 1964. Vroom stresses and focuses on outcomes, and not on needs unlike Maslow and Herzberg. The theory states that the intensity of a tendency to perform in a particular manner is dependent on the intensity of an expectation that the performance will be followed by a definite outcome and on the appeal of the outcome to the individual.

The Expectancy theory states that employee's motivation is an outcome of how much an individual wants a reward (Valence), the assessment that the likelihood that the effort will lead to expected performance (Expectancy) and the belief that the performance will lead to reward (Instrumentality). In short, Valence is the significance associated by an individual about the expected outcome. It is an expected and not the actual satisfaction that an employee expects to receive after achieving the goals. Expectancy is the faith that better efforts will result in better performance. Expectancy is influenced by factors such as possession of appropriate skills for performing the job, availability of right resources, availability of crucial information and getting the required support for completing the job.

Instrumentality is the faith that if you perform well, then a valid outcome will be there. Instrumentality is affected by factors such as believe in the people who decide who receives what outcome, the simplicity of the process deciding who gets what outcome, and clarity of relationship between performance and outcomes. Thus, the expectancy theory concentrates on the following three relationships:

Effort-performance relationship: What is the likelihood that the individual's effort be recognized in his performance appraisal?

Performance-reward relationship: It talks about the extent to which the employee believes that getting a good performance appraisal leads to organizational rewards.

Rewards-personal goals relationship: It is all about the attractiveness or appeal of the potential reward to the individual.

Vroom was of view that employees consciously decide whether to perform or not at the job. This decision solely depended on the employee's motivation level which in turn depends on three factors of expectancy, valence and instrumentality.

Advantages of the Expectancy Theory

It is based on self-interest individual who want to achieve maximum satisfaction and who wants to minimize dissatisfaction.

This theory stresses upon the expectations and perception; what is real and actual is immaterial.

It emphasizes on rewards or pay-offs.

It focuses on psychological extravagance where final objective of individual is to attain maximum pleasure and least pain.

Limitations of the Expectancy Theory

The expectancy theory seems to be idealistic because quite a few individuals perceive high degree correlation between performance and rewards.

The application of this theory is limited as reward is not directly correlated with performance in many organizations. It is related to other parameters also such as position, effort, responsibility, education, etc.

Implications of the Expectancy Theory

- The managers can correlate the preferred outcomes to the aimed performance levels.
- The managers must ensure that the employees can achieve the aimed performance levels.
- The deserving employees must be rewarded for their exceptional performance.
- The reward system must be fair and just in an organization.
- Organizations must design interesting, dynamic and challenging jobs.
- The employee's motivation level should be continually assessed through various techniques such as questionnaire, personal interviews, etc.

- **McClelland's Theory of Needs**

David McClelland and his associates proposed McClelland's theory of Needs / Achievement Motivation Theory. This theory states that human behaviour is affected by three needs - Need for Power, Achievement and Affiliation. Need for **achievement** is the urge to excel, to accomplish in relation to a set of standards, to struggle to achieve success. Need for **power** is the desire to influence other individual's behaviour as per your wish. In other words, it is the desire to have control over others and to be influential. Need for **affiliation** is a need for open and sociable interpersonal relationships. In other words, it is a desire for relationship based on co-operation and mutual understanding.

The individuals with high achievement needs are highly motivated by competing and challenging work. They look for promotional opportunities in job. They have a strong urge for feedback on their achievement. Such individuals try to get satisfaction in performing things better. High achievement is directly related to high performance. Individuals who are better and above average performers are highly motivated. They assume responsibility for solving the problems at work. McClelland called such individuals as gamblers as they set challenging targets

for themselves and they take deliberate risk to achieve those set targets. Such individuals look for innovative ways of performing job. They perceive achievement of goals as a reward, and value it more than a financial reward.

The individuals who are motivated by power have a strong urge to be influential and controlling. They want that their views and ideas should dominate and thus, they want to lead. Such individuals are motivated by the need for reputation and self-esteem. Individuals with greater power and authority will perform better than those possessing less power. Generally, managers with high need for power turn out to be more efficient and successful managers. They are more determined and loyal to the organization they work for. Need for power should not always be taken negatively. It can be viewed as the need to have a positive effect on the organization and to support the organization in achieving it's goals.

The individuals who are motivated by affiliation have an urge for a friendly and supportive environment. Such individuals are effective performers in a team. These people want to be liked by others. The manager's ability to make decisions is hampered if they have a high affiliation need as they prefer to be accepted and liked by others, and this weakens their objectivity. Individuals having high affiliation needs prefer working in an environment providing greater personal interaction. Such people have a need to be on the good books of all. They generally cannot be good leaders.

✓   **Goal Setting Theory of Motivation**

In 1960's, **Edwin Locke** put forward the Goal-setting theory of motivation. This theory states that goal setting is essentially linked to task performance. It states that specific and challenging goals along with appropriate feedback contribute to higher and better task performance. In simple words, goals indicate and give direction to an employee about what needs to be done and how much efforts are required to be put in. The important **features of goal-setting theory** are as follows:

The willingness to work towards attainment of goal is main source of job motivation. Clear, particular and difficult goals are greater motivating factors than easy, general and vague goals.

Specific and clear goals lead to greater output and better performance. Unambiguous, measurable and clear goals accompanied by a deadline for completion avoids misunderstanding.

Goals should be **realistic and challenging**. This gives an individual a feeling of pride and triumph when he attains them, and sets him up for attainment of next goal. The more challenging the goal, the greater is the reward generally and the more is the passion for achieving it.

Better and appropriate feedback of results directs the employee behaviour and contributes to higher performance than absence of feedback. Feedback is a means of gaining reputation, making clarifications and regulating goal difficulties. It helps employees to work with more involvement and leads to greater job satisfaction.

Employees' participation in goal is not always desirable.

Participation of setting goal, however, makes goal more acceptable and leads to more involvement.

Goal setting theory has certain eventualities such as:

a.   **Self-efficiency-** Self-efficiency is the individual's self-confidence and faith that he has potential of performing the task. Higher the level of self-efficiency, greater will be the efforts put in by the individual when they face challenging tasks. While, lower the level of self-efficiency, less will be the efforts put in by the individual or he might even quit while meeting challenges.

b.   **Goal commitment-** Goal setting theory assumes that the individual is committed to the goal and will not leave the goal. The goal commitment is dependent on the following factors:

i.   Goals are made open, known and broadcasted.
ii. Goals should be set-self by individual rather than designated.
iii. Individual's set goals should be consistent with the organizational goals and vision.

Advantages of Goal Setting Theory

•   Goal setting theory is a technique used to raise incentives for employees to complete work quickly and effectively.

- Goal setting leads to better performance by increasing motivation and efforts, but also through increasing and improving the feedback quality.

Limitations of Goal Setting Theory

- At times, the organizational goals are in conflict with the managerial goals. Goal conflict has a detrimental effect on the performance if it motivates incompatible action drift.
- Very difficult and complex goals stimulate riskier behaviour.
- If the employee lacks skills and competencies to perform actions essential for goal, then the goal-setting can fail and lead to undermining of performance.
- There is no evidence to prove that goal-setting improves job satisfaction.

Reinforcement Theory of Motivation

Reinforcement theory of motivation was proposed by BF Skinner and his associates. It states that individual's behaviour is a function of its consequences. It is based on "law of effect", i.e, individual's behaviour with positive consequences tends to be repeated, but individual's behaviour with negative consequences tends not to be repeated.

Reinforcement theory of motivation overlooks the internal state of individual, i.e., the inner feelings and drives of individuals are ignored by Skinner. This theory focuses totally on what happens to an individual when he takes some action. Thus, according to Skinner, the external environment of the organization must be designed effectively and positively so as to motivate the employee. This theory is a strong tool for analyzing controlling mechanism for individual's behaviour. However, it does not focus on the causes of individual's behaviour.

The managers use the following methods for controlling the behaviour of the employees:

Positive Reinforcement- This implies giving a positive response when an individual shows positive and required behaviour. For example - Immediately praising an employee for coming early for job. This will increase probability of outstanding behaviour occurring again.

Reward is a positive reinforce, but not necessarily. If and only if the employees' behaviour improves, reward can said to be a positive reinforcer. Positive reinforcement stimulates occurrence of a behaviour. It must be noted that more spontaneous is the giving of reward, the greater reinforcement value it has.

Negative Reinforcement- This implies rewarding an employee by removing negative / undesirable consequences. Both positive and negative reinforcement can be used for increasing desirable / required behaviour.

Punishment- It implies removing positive consequences so as to lower the probability of repeating undesirable behaviour in future. In other words, punishment means applying undesirable consequence for showing undesirable behaviour. For instance - Suspending an employee for breaking the organizational rules. Punishment can be equalized by positive reinforcement from alternative source.

Extinction- It implies absence of reinforcements. In other words, extinction implies lowering the probability of undesired behaviour by removing reward for that kind of behaviour. For instance - if an employee no longer receives praise and admiration for his good work, he may feel that his behaviour is generating no fruitful consequence. Extinction may unintentionally lower desirable behaviour.

Implications of Reinforcement Theory

Reinforcement theory explains in detail how an individual learns behaviour. Managers who are making attempt to motivate the employees must ensure that they do not reward all employees simultaneously. They must tell the employees what they are not doing correct. They must tell the employees how they can achieve positive reinforcement.

McClelland's Theory of Needs

David McClelland and his associates proposed McClelland's theory of Needs / Achievement Motivation Theory. This theory states that human behaviour is affected by three needs - Need for Power, Achievement and Affiliation. Need for **achievement** is the urge to excel, to accomplish in relation to a set of standards, to struggle to achieve success. Need for **power** is the desire to influence other individual's behaviour as per your wish. In other words, it is the desire to have control over others and to be influential. Need for **affiliation** is a need for open and sociable interpersonal relationships. In other words, it is a desire for relationship based on co-operation and mutual understanding.

The individuals with high achievement needs are highly motivated by competing and challenging work. They look for promotional opportunities in job. They have a strong urge for feedback on their achievement. Such individuals try to get satisfaction in performing things better. High achievement is directly related to high performance. Individuals who are better and above average performers are highly motivated. They assume responsibility for solving the problems at work. McClelland called such individuals as gamblers as they set challenging targets

for themselves and they take deliberate risk to achieve those set targets. Such individuals look for innovative ways of performing job. They perceive achievement of goals as a reward, and value it more than a financial reward.

The individuals who are motivated by power have a strong urge to be influential and controlling. They want that their views and ideas should dominate and thus, they want to lead. Such individuals are motivated by the need for reputation and self-esteem. Individuals with greater power and authority will perform better than those possessing less power. Generally, managers with high need for power turn out to be more efficient and successful managers. They are more determined and loyal to the organization they work for. Need for power should not always be taken negatively. It can be viewed as the need to have a positive effect on the organization and to support the organization in achieving it's goals.

The individuals who are motivated by affiliation have an urge for a friendly and supportive environment. Such individuals are effective performers in a team. These people want to be liked by others. The manager's ability to make decisions is hampered if they have a high affiliation need as they prefer to be accepted and liked by others, and this weakens their objectivity. Individuals having high affiliation needs prefer working in an environment providing greater personal interaction. Such people have a need to be on the good books of all. They generally cannot be good leaders.

✓ **Reinforcement Theory of Motivation**

Reinforcement theory of motivation was proposed by BF Skinner and his associates. It states that individual's behaviour is a function of its consequences. It is based on "law of effect", i.e, individual's behaviour with positive consequences tends to be repeated, but individual's behaviour with negative consequences tends not to be repeated.

Reinforcement theory of motivation overlooks the internal state of individual, i.e., the inner feelings and drives of individuals are ignored by Skinner. This theory focuses totally on what happens to an individual when he takes some action. Thus, according to Skinner, the external environment of the organization must be designed effectively and positively so as to motivate the employee. This theory is a strong tool for analyzing controlling mechanism for individual's behaviour. However, it does not focus on the causes of individual's behaviour.

The managers use the following methods for controlling the behaviour of the employees:

Positive Reinforcement- This implies giving a positive response when an individual shows positive and required behaviour. For example - Immediately praising an employee for coming early for job. This will increase probability of outstanding behaviour occurring again. Reward is a positive reinforce, but not necessarily. If and only if the employees' behaviour improves, reward can said to be a positive reinforcer. Positive reinforcement stimulates occurrence of a behaviour. It must be noted that more spontaneous is the giving of reward, the greater reinforcement value it has.

Negative Reinforcement- This implies rewarding an employee by removing negative / undesirable consequences. Both positive and negative reinforcement can be used for increasing desirable / required behaviour.

Punishment- It implies removing positive consequences so as to lower the probability of repeating undesirable behaviour in future. In other words, punishment means applying undesirable consequence for showing undesirable behaviour. For instance - Suspending an employee for breaking the organizational rules. Punishment can be equalized by positive reinforcement from alternative source.

Extinction- It implies absence of reinforcements. In other words, extinction implies lowering the probability of undesired behaviour by removing reward for that kind of behaviour. For instance - if an employee no longer receives praise and admiration for his good work, he may feel that his behaviour is generating no fruitful consequence. Extinction may unintentionally lower desirable behaviour.

Implications of Reinforcement Theory

Reinforcement theory explains in detail how an individual learns behaviour. Managers who are making attempt to motivate the employees must ensure that they do not reward all employees simultaneously. They must tell the employees what they are not doing correct. They must tell the employees how they can achieve positive reinforcement.

Equity Theory of Motivation

The core of the equity theory is the principle of balance or equity. As per this motivation theory, an individual's motivation level is correlated to his perception of equity, fairness and justice practiced by the management. Higher is individual's perception of fairness, greater is the motivation level and vice versa. While evaluating fairness, employee compares the job input (in terms of contribution) to outcome (in terms of compensation) and also compares the same with that of another peer of equal cadre/category. D/I ratio (output-input ratio) is used to make such a comparison.

EQUITY THEORY	
Ratio Comparison	**Perception**
O/I a < O/I b	Under-rewarded (Equity Tension)
O/I a = O/I b	Equity
O/I a > O/I b	Over-rewarded (Equity Tension)

Negative Tension state: Equity is perceived when this ratio is equal. While if this ratio is unequal, it leads to "equity tension". J.Stacy Adams called this a negative tension state which motivates him to do something right to relieve this tension. A comparison has been made between 2 workers A and B to understand this point.

Referents: The four comparisons an employee can make have been termed as "referents" according to Goodman. The referent chosen is a significant variable in equity theory. These referents are as follows:

✓ Self-inside: An employee's experience in a different position inside his present organization.

✓ Self-outside: An employee's experience in a situation outside the present organization.

- ✓ Other-inside: Another employee or group of employees inside the employee's present organization.

- ✓ Other-outside: Another employee or employees outside the employee's present organization.

An employee might compare himself with his peer within the present job in the current organization or with his friend/peer working in some other organization or with the past jobs held by him with others. An employee's choice of the referent will be influenced by the appeal of the referent and the employee's knowledge about the referent.

Moderating Variables: The gender, salary, education and the experience level are moderating variables. Individuals with greater and higher education are more informed. Thus, they are likely to compare themselves with the outsiders. Males and females prefer same sex comparison. It has been observed that females are paid typically less than males in comparable jobs and have less salary expectations than male for the same work. Thus, a women employee that uses another women employee as a referent tends to lead to a lower comparative standard. Employees with greater experience know their organization very well and compare themselves with their own colleagues, while employees with less experience rely on their personal experiences and knowledge for making comparisons.

Choices: The employees who perceive inequity and are under negative tension can make the following choices:

Change in input (e.g. Don't overexert)

Change their outcome (Produce quantity output and increasing earning by sacrificing quality when piece rate incentive system exist)

Choose a different referent

Quit the job

Change self perception (For instance - I know that I've performed better and harder than everyone else.)

Change perception of others (For instance - Jack's job is not as desirable as I earlier thought it was.)

Assumptions of the Equity Theory

- The theory demonstrates that the individuals are concerned both with their own rewards and also with what others get in their comparison.

- Employees expect a fair and equitable return for their contribution to their jobs.

- Employees decide what their equitable return should be after comparing their inputs and outcomes with those of their colleagues.

- Employees who perceive themselves as being in an inequitable scenario will attempt to reduce the inequity either by distorting inputs and/or outcomes psychologically, by directly altering inputs and/or outputs, or by quitting the organization.

Expectancy Theory of Motivation

The expectancy theory was proposed by **Victor Vroom** of Yale School of Management in 1964. Vroom stresses and focuses on outcomes, and not on needs unlike Maslow and Herzberg. The theory states that the intensity of a tendency to perform in a particular manner is dependent on the intensity of an expectation that the performance will be followed by a definite outcome and on the appeal of the outcome to the individual.

The **Expectancy theory** states that employee's motivation is an outcome of how much an individual wants a reward (Valence), the assessment that the likelihood that the effort will lead to expected performance (Expectancy) and the belief that the performance will lead to reward (Instrumentality). In short, **Valence** is the significance associated by an individual about the expected outcome. It is an expected and not the actual satisfaction that an employee expects to receive after achieving the goals. **Expectancy** is the faith that better efforts will result in better performance. Expectancy is influenced by factors such as possession of appropriate skills for performing the job, availability of right resources, availability of crucial information and getting the required support for completing the job.

Instrumentality is the faith that if you perform well, then a valid outcome will be there. Instrumentality is affected by factors such as believe in the people who decide who receives what outcome, the simplicity of the process deciding who gets what outcome, and clarity of relationship between performance and outcomes. Thus, the expectancy theory concentrates on the following three relationships:

✓ Effort-performance relationship: What is the likelihood that the individual's effort be recognized in his performance appraisal?

114

✓   Performance-reward relationship: It talks about the extent to which the employee believes that getting a good performance appraisal leads to organizational rewards.

✓   Rewards-personal goals relationship: It is all about the attractiveness or appeal of the potential reward to the individual.

Vroom was of view that employees consciously decide whether to perform or not at the job. This decision solely depended on the employee's motivation level which in turn depends on three factors of expectancy, valence and instrumentality.

Advantages of the Expectancy Theory

✓   It is based on self-interest individual who want to achieve maximum satisfaction and who wants to minimize dissatisfaction.

✓   This theory stresses upon the expectations and perception; what is real and actual is immaterial.

✓   It emphasizes on rewards or pay-offs.

✓   It focuses on psychological extravagance where final objective of individual is to attain maximum pleasure and least pain.

Limitations of the Expectancy Theory

✓   The expectancy theory seems to be idealistic because quite a few individuals perceive high degree correlation between performance and rewards.

✓   The application of this theory is limited as reward is not directly correlated with performance in many organizations. It is related to other parameters also such as position, effort, responsibility, education, etc.

Implications of the Expectancy Theory

✓ The managers can correlate the preferred outcomes to the aimed performance levels.

✓ The managers must ensure that the employees can achieve the aimed performance levels.

✓ The deserving employees must be rewarded for their exceptional performance.

✓ The reward system must be fair and just in an organization.

✓ Organizations must design interesting, dynamic and challenging jobs.

✓ The employee's motivation level should be continually assessed through various techniques such as questionnaire, personal interviews, etc.